BEYOND THE MAGIC PILL

A Collection of the Insights of Illusions

By

Odille Rault

First Printing: June 2012

ISBN: 978-1477646793

TABLE OF CONTENTS

INTRODUCTION 5

THE MAGIC PILL.. 7

   It's All You! 7

   Why Don't You Grant Your Wishes? 10

   You Don't Have to Love Yourself!... 12

   The Magic Pill... 14

THE SECOND DOSE 16

   What About the "Bad" Stuff We've Created?............................... 16

   The Hall of Mirrors... 18

   Taking The Magic Pill, and Still Scared?................................... 19

   No Need to Run Screaming… 21

   The Magic Phrase 23

WHY "LOVE YOUR NEIGHBOR AS YOU LOVE YOURSELF" IS
MISLEADING.. 25

THE SLIDING DOORS TO WHAT
YOU WANT 26

I HATE MY JOB – SHOULD I LEAVE? 28

WHAT IF IT FEELS GOOD TO JUST WATCH TV ALL DAY? 30

THE ROOT OF ALL EVIL... 32

HIGH SELF ESTEEM EQUALS TRUE HUMILITY...................... 36

THE KEY TO HAPPINESS - TURNING INSIDE OUT 38

WHEN YOU WONDER "HOW/WHY/
WHEN DID I ATTRACT THIS?!"... 39

WHY ARE RESULTS TAKING SO LONG? 41

HE'S SO POSITIVE, BELIEVES HE LIVES ACCORDING TO
THE LOA... AND YET, HE'S STILL SKINT 45

WHY DO SOME PEOPLE STRUGGLE AND
OTHERS DON'T?.. 48

AN INTERESTING PERSPECTIVE 51

GETTING PAST STUBBORN NEGATIVE BELIEFS 54

A VERY SIMPLE WAY TO KEEP POSITIVE 58

DEALING WITH DOUBTS AND WORRIES 60

Dealing With Doubts and Worries Q & A... 62

THE DOG WHISPERER METHOD OF
CHANGING THOUGHT PATTERNS 64

RESPECT, SELF ESTEEM AND THE DOG WHISPERER! 67

THE LOA TREASURE HUNT TRAIL TO WHAT YOU WANT 69

A TALE OF TWO COUNTRIES...71

THE TRUTH ABOUT FEELING SORRY FOR YOURSELF.....................74

Feeling Sorry for Yourself Q & A.. 77

IF YOU CAN'T STOP BEING HARD ON YOURSELF 89

IF YOU FEEL YOU CAN'T STOP STRUGGLING 91

PARENTING - PAYING IT BACKWARDS!...95

YOU HAVE A SUPERPOWER!...107

How to Use Your Superpower.. 109

DEALING WITH THE "DON'T WANTS" 115

Fear of aiming Unconditional Love at "don't wants" -
isn't that encouraging more of them? 117

Superpower Q & A.. 121

IF YOU CAN'T BE WITH THE THINGS YOU LOVE, LOVE THE
THINGS YOU HATE..126

HOW OTHERS TREAT YOU IS THEIR KARMA,
HOW YOU REACT IS YOURS..128

HOW TO CHANGE OTHER PEOPLE'S ATTITUDE,
BEHAVIOR AND ACTIONS...131

UNCONDITIONAL LOVE AND BULLYING – A TEENAGER'S
EXPERIENCE 135

EXERCISES AND EXPERIMENTS 140

CONCLUSION..149

REFERENCES AND RESOURCES: 150

Introduction

Hi there ☺

Before you go any further, I feel it's important to warn you about the style in which this book is written. I have chosen to write in a conversational style rather than a formal editorial one. I find it easier and more effective to get what I want to say across, writing in this way. The other reason is that most of what is in this book was originally written as posts on forums, and I felt that if I changed that, the essence of the messages wouldn't get through - hence the casual writing tone and expressions, and unconventional grammar. And a lot of sentences starting with "and" ;)

So, I'm hoping that the lack of formal tone (and the inclusion of smiley and winking faces… along with the odd "lol") won't put you off, and that you'll be able to take it in the fun way it's meant, as well as absorb the messages and insights.

Why the book?

Over the past six years I've written many posts on forums, and coached many people in overcoming a wide variety of challenges. Having gone through an immense amount of self development myself, I've loved helping those who want to change their lives – and the feedback has been wonderfully rewarding.

Over the course of the last three years or so, several people have suggested I put all of the information I've written into a book – a compilation of posts and letters. Well, I finally got around to it, and here it is! ☺ My username on the forums is "Illusions" – which explains the subtitle of this book. "The Magic Pill" and "The Second Dose" are two little ebooks I wrote a few years ago, which have helped hundreds of people improve their lives and overcome challenges. I've included these as the first two chapters of this book.

What the....??

Not all of the information here will resonate with every reader, but I'm hoping that you will find at least one or two insights that will empower you to achieve the improvements you want to make in your life. The main message I want to get across through all of this information is: **You have complete power over what you experience in your life, and no-one else can affect that without your permission.** Now, that may sound far-fetched – and even ridiculous – but my intention is that by the time you've read through this book, you'll see, not only why that is the truth, but also how to use that power consciously.

Been there, done that.

Everything I write about is a result of changes I've made in my own life. I've been through a lot of hair-raising challenges and, as I've found solutions for myself, I've shared what I've discovered by writing about it. This is a culmination of the tools and insights that have led to my being happier than I've ever been before – I hope that at least some of it leads you to the same result! ☺

You'll need an open mind, and a willingness to adjust your beliefs and perspective in order to make the changes you wish to see in your life. Having said that, if some of it seems too far-fetched for you, even with an open mind, just take on board what does make sense to you, and leave what sounds too weird ;)

At the back of this book, you'll find a list of resources for further reading on some of the topics I touch on. There are also a few exercises and challenges for those with an adventurous and fun streak! ;)

Enjoy!

Love and Light and Magic xxx

The Magic Pill

It's All You!

This chapter is a **very brief** introduction to the Law of Attraction. If you wish to find out more about the LOA, you can find a lot more detail through the movie or book <u>The Secret, Abraham-Hicks,</u> and on the <u>Powerful Intentions Forums</u> – as well as many other books and websites.

So if the Law of Attraction is new to you, and you find yourself confused or "pooh-poohing" the information below, do make a detour to one of these sites, to find out a bit more about it, and get your questions and suspicions answered ;)

For those of you who already know the LOA, that is NOT the Magic Pill. The Magic Pill is NOT the LOA – keep reading ;)

The Simplified Basics of the Law of Attraction as it pertains to the Magic Pill:

You create and attract Everything in your life. Everything. The situations, the people, and every experience. You do this through the rate at which you are vibrating (which is indicated by how you're feeling). You do this automatically. You always have done.

Just like if you walk off a ledge, you'll hit the ground, you don't think about it, you don't have to consciously do anything to hit the ground.

The Law of Gravity does it for you. The Law of Attraction works the same way. No matter who you are, what you do, or what you believe, the Law of Attraction means you attract what you vibrate. (If this sounds a bit "wafty" for you, you'll find a perfectly logical, down-to-earth explanation at the end of this chapter. ;)

"You attract and create that for which you are a vibrational match" Therefore, in order to get what you want, you need to be vibrating in sync with it. You cannot attract abundance while you're vibrating poverty and lack. You also cannot attract poverty and lack while you are vibrating abundance! (handy isn't it ;))

You know how you're vibrating, by the way you're feeling. So, the most important point about the Law of Attraction, as it pertains to the Magic Pill, is the fact that **YOU create and attract everything in your life.** No-one else can create in your life – **you allow or disallow, you create, you attract**.

The Best Thing about this is: the Magic Pill is the **EASIEST, QUICKEST way to create and attract exactly what you want!** Without visualization, without meditation, without "working" on it. There's nothing wrong with visualization and meditation etc. – if you enjoy it. But it's not **necessary.**

Can't wait to tell you why… …… ;)

≪ ≪ ≪   ≫ ≫ ≫

An Aside:

If the Law of Attraction seems a bit "wafty" to you…

I have many friends who are skeptical about the LOA – and in fact, about anything spiritual, seeing it as "wafty". But excluding Abraham,

The Secret, Quantum Physics etc. there's a perfectly "down-to-earth" explanation.

The life a person is living is a direct result of his or her core beliefs. Our core beliefs affect the choices we make, the actions we take (or don't take), our behavior, and how we relate to others... all of which produce consequences which result in our life circumstances.

Whatever we've been taught, we have the power to choose what we believe. ☺

Why Don't You Grant Your Wishes?

So, if YOU create and attract Everything in your life, why don't you grant all your wishes? Why don't you have all the money and experiences, and love and health and..... well, everything that you want? – especially if you are already aware of the Law of Attraction, and HAVE been visualizing and meditating to become a vibrational match for what you want... why hasn't it "worked"?

Well, it does work – it always works – for EVERYONE (just like the Law of Gravity works for everyone), so there must be some kind of discrepancy in how you're vibrating (feeling). There must be some kind of block – some kind of limiting belief that means that, despite **consciously** focusing on what you want, and feeling good, and visualizing etc. there is some kind of limiting belief hiding in there somewhere.

The great news is: You don't have to find it. You don't have to change it. You don't have to "work on it". You don't have to clear it.

Whatever those limiting beliefs are, the root of them will be low self esteem and self worth. Regardless of whether you think your self esteem is fine, **if you are creating/ attracting any kind of lack in your life, you have low self esteem and low self worth.**

Think about it: You already know you create and attract everything in your life. **So, if you had high self esteem and self worth, why**

would you create any kind of lack for yourself? You would create only abundance.

So ... the answer to receiving abundance in all areas of your life ... is high self esteem and self worth.

The FASTEST, EASIEST (and I believe, the ONLY) way to increase your self esteem and self worth is to experience self love......

But I'd said this would be EASY. So.... **you don't have to love yourself!**

You Don't Have to Love Yourself!

I've read and heard for years that I should "love myself", and that the key to everything is "self love"... And it always felt really difficult and awkward and uncomfortable, and even "wafty". And I didn't know **how** to "love myself" And I even thought "Well I *do* love myself." – although that was kinda intellectual rather than emotional ;)

And then I realized ..... **We don't have to "love ourselves"** – we ALREADY love ourselves. What we need to do, is NOTICE and RECOGNIZE that we love ourselves – and how much! And the more we notice and recognize how much we love ourselves, the more the expression of that love INCREASES – and the more noticeable it becomes.

It struck me that throughout our lives, we've developed blocks against the love we have for ourselves. So, although the love is there, and it always has been, we block it out. We've been taught to deny it, to hide it, and we fail to recognize it. So **we create diversions from it.**

So, the answer is much **easier** than **actively trying** to love yourself. All you have to do is **recognize** that **you already do.** Deep deep down inside. You were born with love for yourself. And the **evidence** is in every good thing in your life. **Every good thing that happens** – no matter how small – is **evidence you already love yourself.** And as you start to recognize that, each time you recognize it, you open the block a little. Each time you recognize it, you feel the warm fuzzy tingle that will raise your vibrations, and expand your energy, and open the block more each time. And it picks up momentum as you go ;)

And your memory of your love for yourself will begin to come back.

The Magic Pill

And heeeeeere it is …… the Ultimate Answer to Everything … ….

…. Okay, so it's not an actual pill, but it is even EASIER than taking a pill – and it's certainly magic!

You already know that you create and attract everything in your life. So, every thing and person in your life that makes you feel good – is an expression of love from yourself, to yourself. Just like we give and do things for others that make them feel good, as an expression of our love for them – we do the same for ourselves. Every sunny day, smile from a stranger, convenient parking spot – every thing that goes your way – is an expression of love **from yourself, to yourself** – a way in which you are expressing your love for yourself. The more you **Recognize** this, the more you will automatically open up and **allow** more of these expressions of love into your life, and you will see them **increase** – **Daily!**

The result is, you get more and more and more of what makes you feel good – whatever that may be – AUTOMATICALLY!

So, here are the directions for the Magic Pill:

This is all you have to do: (if you've skipped all the other chapters, then this is not all you need to do – you also need to read the other chapters ;)

Start noticing every single thing in your life that makes you feel good, and **Recognize** each one **as an expression of love from yourself, to yourself.** The most important part of this is the second part – the **recognizing YOU** created that as an expression of love for **YOURSELF.**

The result of this will be: Your Self Esteem and Self Worth will Soar! Firstly, because you are recognizing YOUR power – YOU create everything in your life. Aren't you clever! ☺ And Secondly: imagine how much you must love yourself – to be constantly expressing that love and finding so many different ways to make yourself feel good! **There is nothing more Powerful than realizing that you are Worthy of a Love as Great as Your Own!** Now THAT'S a REAL Self Esteem and Self Worth Booster!!

Start now. See how many expressions of love from yourself, to yourself, you can spot today. You don't have to list them (although you can if you wish), all you have to do is notice and RECOGNIZE – that's all. The rest is AUTOMATIC.

Told you it was Easy ;)

.... one more thing…

Whenever you catch yourself feeling worry, fear or doubt, remind yourself:

"Oh yes, I remember now – there's no reason to worry because I now know that **I can ONLY create and attract situations and people that make me feel good and that are good for me** – now that I remember that I love myself. And even though this *appears* to be cause for worry, I know it HAS to turn out to be good – it has no choice - because that's ALL I can create/ attract now!"

≪ ≪ ≪ ≫ ≫ ≫

The Second Dose

What About the "Bad" Stuff We've Created?

When I first started taking The Magic Pill, I simply chose to ignore the "bad" things I'd created – to just not look at them for the moment, because I couldn't think of a reason for them or how they fitted in, so I ignored them and only focused on the expressions of love.

However, I was asked by a few people who had read The Magic Pill "What about the "bad" stuff? If I create and attract everything in my life, and I love myself, why have I created and attracted these awful situations/ people?"

This inspired me to look more closely at this point, and when I did, I realized that the "bad" things we've created and attracted into our lives are the **result of blocking out the love we have for ourselves**.

The **resistance** (and in many cases quite <u>aggressive</u> resistance) **to acknowledging/remembering our self-love** is the cause of the "bad" stuff we create and attract.

We really **are conditioned very toxically** against self-love.

Once we start noticing and recognizing that we *do* love ourselves, and as we acknowledge the expressions of that love, **we open up to accept it,** and **thereby, dissolve the blocks and resistance.** And through that, **we no longer have the "bad" side-effects of those blocks.**

Then we can say - and trust it completely - **"I now only create and attract situations and people that make me feel good and that are good for me."**

Because I now know that I love myself, I can **only** create "good" for me.

Since this change in perspective, I have had many occasions when I've started to worry - when something has appeared to be a problem - but I've reminded myself that I now only create and attract situations and people that make me feel good, and that are good for me - and EVERY time it's turned out to be nothing to worry about!

Before I discovered The Magic Pill, I didn't know that the **"bad" things were caused** by the **block against recognizing love for myself**. So therefore, no matter how positive I was, how much I tried to "feel good", how much I tried to "look on the bright side", how much I tried to clear those blocks with various methods, how much I tried ..... well, everything I came across ...... I was still (unknowingly) **blocking self-love!**

Now that the block is dissolving, and I am seeing more and more evidence of how much I love myself - and I'm acknowledging that that's what it is - NOW I know that I **can't create "bad" stuff anymore. It's just not possible** ☺

The Hall of Mirrors

Imagine you were born and raised in one of those carnival Halls of Mirrors - the ones that distort your reflection. So, everywhere around you, is a distorted image of you. You don't know it's distorted - you've never seen any other image of yourself.

Then you go outside, and there you see other people - who all look so good. And you compare yourself to them. And you say "What's wrong with me! Why can't I be like that? Why can't I be like them? They're so.......... and I'm so............."

And you don't know that you are **perfect** - because **you've only ever seen your reflection in the Hall of Mirrors.**

The mirrors in the Hall of Mirrors are the fears and beliefs of certain people around you growing up, and the beliefs and experiences you've collected - and everything else that shapes your self image from birth onwards.

To find out what you're REALLY like, you need to Trust, and notice and recognize the evidence around you of how much you love yourself.

And then you'll realize that when you stepped outside - those were not other people - those were REAL mirrors - showing **Accurate Reflections** of YOU! You just didn't recognize yourself at first! :)

Taking The Magic Pill, and Still Scared?

The following analogy stands for all of the things you're looking at right now, that appear to be "bad" - lack of money, judgment from others, confrontations, things that appear to be "going wrong" and all other "monsters".

I'm sure you've had times when, lying in bed, in the dark, you've seen a shape that you could swear was something - a person, a monster, a.... whatever... but it's not. It turns out to be a robe hanging on the door, or a lamp - even though, before you switched on the light, you couldn't think of anything "normal" it could be.

That's what worries are now. Now that you know you love yourself, although you still "see" a monster, it WILL turn out to be just a robe on the door - or maybe even a person you love - it's just that they look like a monster in the dark - because you can't see them properly – and you **fear** a monster.

As you get closer, and the light increases, you'll find out that what you thought was something to worry about turns out to be nothing - as you keep reminding yourself that you only create good now.

The only thing to fear is fear - because, what you **feel** is what is creating and attracting. So if you don't fear, there's nothing to fear - because you CAN'T create something to fear, without feeling the fear first ;) (There's a nice little tongue-twister☺)

And the way to keep from feeling the fear, is to keep reminding yourself: "**I love myself, so I now only create and attract situations and people that make me feel good, and that are good for me.**"

And then look at all the **evidence** of how much you love yourself - every thing and person that makes you feel good ☺

Trust yourself - you love you. You won't let anything "bad" happen to you - **even though it might look that way until the light comes on ;)**

No Need to Run Screaming…

I think this applies mostly to people who are worrying about lack of money and too many bills.....

Someone recently described their worries about bills and lack of money as being in the sea, surrounded by sharks, waiting for a lifeboat that never seems to arrive.

Not only is the lifeboat just out of sight (**and you probably won't recognize it when it comes**, because it **won't necessarily look the way you imagine** a lifeboat to look;) - but MOST IMPORTANTLY - **those are not sharks!**

They just **look** like sharks! **Very convincing.... but not sharks**. I don't know if you saw the movie "Jaws", but even if you didn't, you may have seen the trailer, or something similar. When you watch a movie like that, **every cell in your body reacts as if you're in danger.**

The only thing that stops you from running screaming into the street, is your conscious mind knowing it's a movie!

But still - even though you KNOW it's just a movie - that shark, or whatever it is, appears **SO real that your whole being** except for a tiny percentage - **reacts as if it IS real!**

So no matter how convincing those "sharks" look - keep reminding yourself - they're not real sharks, they're just really well disguised ;) You can relax a bit. Even though the rest of you is doing its "fight or flight" thing - your conscious mind can keep reminding the rest of you "It's only a movie, **I would NEVER create real sharks for myself**, so I'm just going to have a swim while I wait for the boat!"

"I can now ONLY create and attract situations and people that make me feel good, and that are good for me!"

The Magic Phrase

Here's a phrase which is incredibly simple, but Highly Powerful - to add to the Magic Pill information above.

"Look how much I love myself!"

As you're becoming aware of every good thing you've manifested/ created/ attracted (and bearing in mind that every good thing in your life HAS been manifested/ created/ attracted by You) - when you notice each thing, say to yourself "Look how much I love myself!"

The fact that it's not raining when you have to go out; the fact that you have a car; the fact that you are able to buy milk; the fact that you have a store nearby; the fact that you have a television; the fact that you have a computer; the fact that you have shoes; the fact that the traffic light turned green as you got there; the fact that you have somewhere to live; the fact that you have a loved-one; the fact that you're not in pain; the fact that you're not cold; the fact that there are birds tweeting outside; the fact that you can turn on a tap and get clean running water.... I could go on, but you get the idea ;) - for every good thing you notice in your life (and it takes awareness for this because we - being human - tend to not notice the simple good things in our lives, unless they're no longer there ;)) - for each good thing you notice during your day, say to yourself "Look how much I love myself!".

Notice how you feel when you say that.

And this short phrase works in two ways, on two levels...

1. It lifts and helps to maintain your life state – meaning you are in that moment **attracting more of what makes you feel like that**

2. When you daydream about what you want - about your desires - as you daydream and imagine what it's like to have them... say to yourself "Look how much I love myself!" - **That phrase is now connected to the things you already have that you appreciate**... making it extremely Powerful and Magical in manifesting. It's a **Magical wand** that you are pointing at your target desires ;) They are then endowed with **the same energy as the things that already exist in your life**.

≪ ≪ ≪ ≫ ≫ ≫

Why "Love Your Neighbor as You Love Yourself" is Misleading....

I heard someone quote this phrase from the bible, on the radio yesterday, and I was struck by what is wrong with it...

Most of us show less love, consideration, compassion and courtesy to ourselves than we show anyone else! If we were to love our neighbor as we love ourselves, we would show them no love at all! ;)

I like to switch the phrase around: "Love yourself as you love your neighbor" ;)

≪≪≪ ≫≫≫

The Sliding Doors To What You Want

This is an analogy that helped me understand the difference between focusing on something and allowing it - and focusing on something and keeping it out....I've found that often, if you want something REALLY badly, the way to get it is to take your focus off it for a while, and then it will come to you - **Automatically.**

I know that sounds wonky - and the opposite to what we think we need to do, but here's why I'm suggesting it: When we **desperately** want something, we tend to **grab onto it** and not want to let go, no matter what. This can actually block whatever it is we're holding on to - because the governing underlying vibration in this case, is **Fear** . Fear of losing whatever it is we're holding on to. And it is our **Vibration** that creates and attracts. If our vibration is Fear of not getting what we want.... that is, of course, exactly what we're creating.

Everything (EVERYTHING!) you want is waiting for you just the other side of a pair of sliding doors. And it's just waiting for those doors to slide open so that it can be allowed in.

It is ONLY our vibration that creates and attracts. And low vibrations - like fear, longing, wishing, worry etc - keep those doors tightly shut. High vibrations, like love, trust and joy, slide the doors open.

As we feel these high vibrations, the doors start sliding open, and if we continue with the high vibrations, the doors continue to slide open, and then become open wide enough to start letting in the stuff we want that's waiting just there. When our vibration changes to low, the doors start to slide closed again, so the opening isn't wide enough for the stuff to start coming into our life.

Now, the important thing to know is that the stuff we want is ALWAYS just there - just the other side of those doors. It doesn't pass by, it doesn't go away. It stays right there, waiting for the doors to open wide enough for it to come through - because it is **magnetically held there** simply by the fact that we want it! So as soon as we raise our vibrations again, and those doors start sliding open again, it's still there waiting.

By taking your focus off the thing you've been hanging on to trying really hard to manifest, and by focusing only on every expression of love from yourself, to yourself you will start opening those doors, and the more you do this, the more the doors will open, and once the opening is wide enough, the stuff you want will Automatically come through it, and into your life!

The "big" you (higher self/expanded self/ God/ the Universe) already knows what you want - from the instant you wanted it (and possibly even before you knew you wanted it) So it is already there - just the other side of those doors. All you have to do is allow the doors to open with your vibration

≪ ≪ ≪ ≫ ≫ ≫

I Hate My Job – Should I Leave?

Your only job is to desire, and then to feel good ;) - to do whatever feels good.

You have the choice whether to continue with this work, or to quit. You choose in every moment. By choosing whether to continue or to quit, you're not choosing the academic result, you are choosing **the result of how you feel.**

In other words, whether you continue or you don't will (strangely I know) make no difference to your life on its own! It will only make a difference to how you are feeling in the moment every day - and thereby make a difference to your future.

So, if you love what you're doing, or you hate what you're doing, the work itself is not creating anything, there will be no result directly from the work itself. The way you are feeling while doing the work is what is creating and attracting in your life.

It's a tricky concept to come to terms with at first because of everything we've "known" up until now ;)

We've been convinced all along that, in order to accomplish anything in the physical world, in order to get a result in the physical world, we have to focus on the physical action - that the only way to get something (if we can get it at all) is through working physically for/at it, with the limited vision we have from the physical perspective.

Now, we're starting to remind ourselves of (amongst other things) the Law of Attraction. The only thing that creates/attracts in your life is the vibration of how you're feeling. If you're in a job you hate, find a way to feel good right now anyway – even change your perspective towards the work and the people you work with, and follow what feels good in the meantime, until you find work that you love.

≪ ≪ ≪ ≫ ≫ ≫

What If It Feels Good to Just Watch TV All Day?

So many of us have spent our adult lives forcing ourselves to do stuff we don't want to do, to put up with things we don't want to put up with, and feeling guilty when we "loaf off". The result of this can be: when suddenly given permission to "do what feels good", some of us will say "Well, what if it feels good to just watch TV all day!" The thought behind that statement is "This is too good to be true ... isn't it?" ;)

The truth is you will ONLY feel good when doing what's good for you. And if watching TV all day feels good right now (genuinely feels good - meaning you feel happy and content), then that is EXACTLY what you need to do right now! Trust me, it won't feel that way forever.

It may well be that you need to relax, unwind and clear yourself of tension and stress, and get used to the feeling of doing what feels good. Maybe you need to get used to allowing yourself to relax without feeling guilty, to look after your own needs - to learn that it's okay to do nothing - if that feels good ☺

Someone once said to me that for a drug addict, getting a fix feels good – but it's obviously not good for him. This was my reply:

The example you use of the drug addict is not really a good one because of course, it's an addiction - and it is self-destructive. Anything that is self-destructive is disguised as feeling "good". But when I say "feel good" I mean the way you feel when listening to your favorite music, the way you feel when you treat yourself to a movie you've been wanting to see, the way you feel in a luxurious bubble bath, the way you feel when you think about what you love, the way you feel when you play a sport you enjoy, the way you feel when you spend time with friends who make you laugh.

That's the kind of "feel good" you want to focus on. For example, just sitting watching TV all day regardless of what's on, is unlikely to feel this way - it'll probably feel more like rebellion, or depression, or lack of motivation, or listlessness. But, watching your favorite TV programs all day may well feel wonderful. It may feel like pampering, like loving yourself, like treating yourself, like cozy, like relaxing, like fun.

And after a period of time, you'll suddenly (or maybe gradually) feel like doing something else - and that will feel good. And step by step - even if it doesn't appear that way - you will be led to your desires, by following your guidance system of what feels good in the moment.

≪ ≪ ≪ ≫ ≫ ≫

The Root of All Evil

Imagine a world in which every person has healthy self esteem, confidence and self worth.

Here's why I believe that low self esteem is at the root of almost all issues, problems and "evil". Let's start from the individual and move out, since that is how life works.

One child is taught to put others before himself. He is taught the feelings of others are more important than his own. He is spoken to with disrespect. His parents are so focused on survival and their own issues that they don't smile or look pleased when they see him. He feels misunderstood because the significant adults in his life don't take the time to really listen to him. Misunderstandings have (on more than a couple of occasions) resulted in punishment and scolding for things that were not his fault, or over which he had no control.

Here are the beliefs that are most likely to be programmed into the child before he even reaches his teen years: "I am not worthy. I am not interesting enough. I am not as important or valuable as others. I am useless." Because these beliefs are **subconscious** it is unlikely they'll ever be discovered unless that child is lucky enough to benefit from therapy or a self development modality that uncovers them.

The **symptoms**, however, will be painfully evident. Unfortunately they won't be recognized as symptoms, they will be seen as problems, issues and evils in their own right.

Combine this child's experience so far, with lack of consistent sufficient sleep and you have a child who, in school, is unable to concentrate resulting in frequently appearing to misbehave (it's often not that he's deliberately going against instructions, it's that his brain was unable to focus enough to either hear and register the instructions or to understand them). Unfortunately the child himself has no idea that this is the case, and simply doesn't know why he is "naughty". The combination of low self worth already thriving in him, along with lack of enough sleep, can also be the reason he's not interested in (or is "bad" at) sport.

So, we now have a child whose self esteem dives even lower due to the experience of being "hopeless" in school and in sport - a fact that is made out to be his fault, but which is, in reality, out of his own control.

This child grows into an adult who has one or more of the following issues resulting directly from a basic program of low self worth and low self esteem: No matter what he does, he seems incapable of making enough money; he always seems to be in relationships that are unhealthy in one way or another; he struggles to find, or succeed in, a career he enjoys and for which he is fairly rewarded; any business he attempts fails. I'm sure you can see how low self esteem and self worth can result in unconscious patterns of undeserving, resentment, self-sabotage, aggression, and attempting to put others down in order to feel better himself.

I believe that most, if not all, "evil" carried out by human beings is the result of a basic drive to feel better about themselves. To those of us with high moral standards that may sound ridiculous, but here's an example: A man attacks another for no apparent reason. The result he's looking for is to feel better about himself. Attacking someone else may make him feel that he's "stronger", or he may have released some of the mental pain he has, or he may have released frustration, or he may feel superior. He feels better now than he did before. He feels above at least one person - his victim.

A teenage girl cuts herself. The result she's looking for: to feel better, because the pain from the cut distracts - at least temporarily - from the pain of what is going on emotionally or mentally.

Imagine the child mentioned earlier, growing up with healthy self esteem and self worth. He's confident that he's interesting and valuable, and a good person because his parents' faces light up when he enters the room. He now has a subconscious belief that he lights up a room when he enters it - which is why, as an adult, he WILL light up a room when he enters it.

He gets enough sleep consistently and eats reasonably healthily enabling him to focus in school and to function at his best, with plenty of energy and coordination in sport. Watch that self esteem and confidence climb!

The adult that child becomes has no need to pull others down in order to feel better. He is emotionally self-sufficient. He is programmed to know that he deserves, and therefore he automatically creates for himself, a fulfilling life including healthy choices in relationships, finances and career. He's comfortable giving to, and doing for, others because he is confident and fulfilled himself. He knows that when someone else receives, it takes nothing away from him.

Can you imagine a whole generation growing up with healthy self esteem and self worth? Can you imagine those people running countries and businesses? Can you imagine a world where each person feels so secure in themselves that they feel no threat from others doing well; where each person feels secure enough to build for themselves, the life they want, doing what they enjoy; where each person is capable of making themselves financially secure and building healthy relationships; and where each person is relaxed and secure enough to show love to others without feeling vulnerable or weak.

I believe that low self esteem is the root of all evil.

≪ ≪ ≪ ≫ ≫ ≫

High Self Esteem Equals True Humility

It may sound contradictory to many people, but there is logic to it...

High self esteem (genuine high self esteem, not inflated ego - that would be low self esteem ;)) means **knowing for certain** that you are deserving, loved, loveable, secure, safe... and so on. This in turn results in not needing to hang onto stuff/ people/ experiences. It also comes with the knowledge that you can't get what you think you need - from someone else.

It also means that you're happy for others to be as they are, do and say what they do and say, and to believe whatever they believe because nothing they do can threaten or take away from you.

Practical Results of High Self Esteem

High self esteem results in financial stability, rewarding relationships, happy work, physical health, and so on - because a person with high self esteem will look after themselves better - in all areas of their life - because they genuinely believe they're worth it. ☺

... I'm getting to the humility bit, bear with me ;) ....

A person with high self esteem has an inbuilt feeling of security, a knowledge that someone else having, doesn't take away from them having. They don't feel threatened by the success (or failure) of others. They have no resentment towards others because they know that **they are perfectly capable of getting whatever it is they need and want.**

This means that they are able to be **genuinely humble**. Low self esteem harbors resentment, greed, fear and jealousy, whereas a person with high self esteem can look at someone who has a skill they admire, and they can feel **truly humbled by it** - because they don't see the fact that they don't have that skill themselves as a weakness, they don't need to have the skill themselves to feel worthy - they can **genuinely admire it in someone else - with true humility, free from any negative undertones or influences**.

I hope this makes sense the way I've described it - it makes sense in my head, but it's tricky to explain it in writing.

Aiming to develop genuine high self esteem will result in a lot more besides true humility of course, and the LOA - if it's interpreted the right way - does a lot to help develop high self esteem. ☺

≪ ≪ ≪ ≫ ≫ ≫

The Key to Happiness...
Turning Inside Out

When Man was created, God decided to hide from him, the key to great success and happiness - the truth of how life as a human really works. He felt that if it were readily available, Man may abuse it. Some of the wiser animals on the planet made suggestions for the most effective hiding places. "Hide it at the bottom of the deepest ocean." recommended the dolphin. "Hide it at the top of the highest mountain." was the owl's contribution. "I will dig deep into the earth," suggested the mole, "and I will bury it right in the center. They'll never find it there."

But God felt certain that Man, with his inquisitive nature, would eventually reach the bottom of the ocean, the top of the highest mountain, and even the center of the earth.

Finally, a squirrel spoke up. "Hide it inside him, for that is the last place he will look."

And that is exactly where it is.

If you believe, as I do, that everything "out there" is a reflection of what is going on inside yourself, you already know that the only efficient way of changing anything in your life, is by changing inside first.

Our bodies and minds are programmed as we grow, according to our experiences. These experiences include personal experience, and what we learn from others. Since each of us experiences life in a unique way, the program running in each person's subconscious, and in every cell of our bodies, is as individual as we are.

≪ ≪ ≪ ≫ ≫ ≫

When You Wonder "How/Why/When Did I Attract THIS?!"...

So, we know that we manifest and attract stuff into our lives, but sometimes it's really difficult to understand how, and sometimes it really doesn't make sense, and sometimes we can't figure out what we're doing that could be attracting that experience.

Here's an analogy I thought of that has really helped me:

We know intellectually (according to what we've learned about the Law of Attraction) that we are the only ones who can create and attract in our lives.

Have you ever looked for something where you thought you'd left it, and discovered it's in a different place - and you cannot remember moving it? "I'm sure I left it there!" But no-one else has been in that room, only you, so it MUST have been you who moved it, you just cannot remember doing it?

What the....???

So, if you think of your life as a room. And you are the only person who can get into that room. No-one has ever been in that room except you. And sometimes you'll notice a window is broken, or there's a stain on the rug, and you think "What the...??? Who did that! Why? How?" and "It wasn't me - I've been cleaning and tidying and looking after this room..."

but then you remember, you're the only person who's been in that room, so it <u>must</u> have been something you did in the past even though you don't remember it... BUT - here's the BEST part of this: **It doesn't** __matter__ what it was that you did to cause this situation, or when, or why, or how... you can just say "Okay, so it must have been something I did, doesn't matter what it was, moving on...." and focus on what you're doing right now.

Starting Now...and Now....and Now ;)

There's no need to work out what you did to cause the broken window, you can just focus on fixing or replacing it (and resist the urge to play baseball in the room from now on ;)) In other words, it doesn't matter how you managed to attract the angry boss, you can just recognize that there must have been some cause you made - doesn't matter what - and just focus on feeling good right now, sending unconditional love to the person and situation and ESPECIALLY to YOURSELF ;)

This way, you're taking your focus off the effects of previous causes (the whys and hows and whos), and focusing on making good causes from this moment - it naturally raises your life-state and therefore what you're attracting right now.

Remind yourself regularly: **"I'm the only one who's been in the room."**

Having said this, it's also very important to keep reminding yourself to be compassionate – with yourself. In other words, when you discover something's "wrong" in your room, and you remind yourself that you're the only one who's been in there, so it must have been something you did in the past... it's very, VERY important to also feel compassion for yourself at that time - whatever it was you did, you didn't know you were doing it, and so you automatically forgive and move on. Again, keeping the focus on creating good causes right now in the moment. ☺

«« « »» »

Why Are Results Taking So Long?

"Why is it taking so long to see results? Sometimes I think things have changed, but then something happens and it's like I'm back to square one!"

Remember, even when you consciously decide to do something, and consciously change a pattern, the 90% of you that is unconscious (programmed, doesn't think for itself) didn't get the memo yet!

It takes a while. There's no way of knowing how long it will take for anyone's subconscious to catch up with their conscious decisions. The only time you'll know is when you see some kind of result - then you'll know, ah, more of me has now caught up ;)

But the good news is: it won't be a case of all 90% all the time. Different aspects will change at different times and it will probably be gradual. And it will be different for different changes.

Coffee vs. Train Crash

Imagine a coffee shop. Every day for the past twenty years, a particular customer has come in at 11am and ordered a black coffee with four sugars. All the staff know him, and he no longer needs to order. As soon as the staff members see him, they make a black coffee with four sugars, and serve it to him.

Then one day, he changes his order. When they bring him the coffee, he tells them he no longer wants sugar in it. Now, the next time he comes in, one of two things happen: either, the same staff member serves him, but is so in the habit of putting four sugars in the coffee, she goes ahead and does it automatically and has to be reminded by the customer - no sugar. Or ... a different staff member - who hasn't been told about the change, will automatically make the coffee - black with four sugars.

So, the time it takes for that customer to automatically get coffee with no sugar depends on how many staff members there are, and what kind of communication exists between them. It will also depend on each staff member, and their own individual ability to get out of the habit, as to how long it will be before it becomes automatic for the customer to receive a black coffee with NO sugar.

During this transition, he may sometimes get black coffee without sugar, and then get four sugars again. Sometimes he may get two sugars, because the staff member caught herself half-way through putting sugar in, and stopped.

But each time he comes in, he's getting closer to what he wants, because each time he comes in and the coffee is made - even when they accidently put sugar in it, the message is getting more and more ingrained.

And then one day, he'll walk in and his coffee will be automatically served without sugar, and the next day, it will happen again.... and so it will become the norm.

Now.... here's another example - and this explains the difference between the subject matter. Imagine a Railway Junction. There are two workers who control the signals at this railway junction. Both have been doing this for twenty years. Every day for twenty years, two trains have come from opposite directions at 4pm. And every day for twenty years, the controller on duty has set the signal for the East-bound train to stop, in order to allow the West-bound train through, before then giving the green signal to the East-bound one.

One day, both controllers receive a message to say there's a new addition to the track, and from now on, they don't need to stop the East-bound train - there is a new track for it.

Now, imagine how long it's going to take for those controllers to trust that new instruction - considering that if it's not true, or if it's an error, the trains will crash and people will be killed.

So in this scenario, unlike the coffee shop where it was just a case of everyone getting the message and getting into the new habit - in this scenario you've got the Danger element as well! And THAT will take longer. These controllers may need to receive that message many times before they believe and trust it.

And one of the controllers may be more trusting than the other, so he may one day allow the train through - and that will work fine. But the other controller may not hear about it, so he may continue to hang onto the old instructions for a while longer - "just in case".

But no matter how long it takes, if he continues to get the message, he will eventually trust that it is true and not a mistake, and/or he will hear about the success from the other controller. And he too will then make the change.

We have no idea of what our cells consider "dangerous" - for example, trusting may feel dangerous - that may be the equivalent to some of our cells, of changing the train signals after all these years.

After allllll these years of not trusting, now suddenly they're told they can trust, well it will take a while for that to get through. Whereas, getting into the habit of noticing the good stuff day-to-day would be more like the coffee shop - a habit change.

So the best thing we can do is to remind ourselves that this is what is happening behind the scenes, and to be patient with ourselves. Know that the message is getting through, and that the results will begin to show as each part of you receives, and trusts the message. The more understanding and patient you are with yourself, the easier and faster the changes will happen because the less stress, the more effective the changes.

So, if you're seeing erratic results, even though you have been changing your thinking and trying so hard..... remember, around 90% of you didn't get the memo yet - some of that 90% may have got it by now, some of it may need to be reminded a few times, and some part of yourself may just need time to trust that it's safe to think that way.

《《《 》》》

He's so positive, believes he lives according to the LOA... and yet, he's still skint

I noticed something about someone close to me recently.

He's very positive, believes in the LOA and buys lottery tickets believing he'll win. He's helpful and generous, and one of the things he looks forward to most when he has a lot of money, is helping others - sharing his wealth with them.....

Here's what I realized the other day - can't believe it never occurred to me before:

The main reason he gives for not doing/ having/ being - is lack of "finances" - "When we have finances, we'll go... do.... be....". "We can't because of lack of finances".... "Finances won't allow..."... and so on. BUT... I don't mean he's negative when he says this - he says it because that's the reality right now - and he is **positive** about getting those "finances" - he has **great faith** that he will get that money - and then he has wonderful plans for it - giving to family and friends, helping those who need it, romantic dinners, doing fun stuff, getting fit and healthy (a gym costs money), eating healthily (healthy food costs money), taking friends out... and all the other things.

And yes, it's a fact that at the moment, the "reality" in the physical world is that there is no money available to him - apart from the basics. However.....

Here's what I noticed the other day.... "Lack of finances" has <u>become part of his reality</u> - and there are two main points here:

1. Because this has become part of his reality, he believes it to be true and reinforces it without realizing it (because of his positive attitude and belief that he will have money, he is under the impression that's what he's creating), he will continue to create exactly what "is" - because that is what now identifies him and his life experience (without his realizing it).

2. "Lack of finances" has become an excuse (although he genuinely doesn't see it that way) for not doing things. There are many people who don't have much money, who still do what they want to - get things done - make the changes they want to make. If he did come into money, it would mean he no longer has the excuse (which I believe is based in a lack of confidence in himself and/or a fear of success and/or failure) - which his subconscious is well aware of and therefore will strive to keep the status quo in order to stay "safe".

If this person starts "acting as if" - and by that I don't mean spending money he hasn't got, I mean doing things anyway in a way that doesn't cost money (a romantic meal at home instead of in a restaurant; a run instead of the gym; just spending good times with friends instead of waiting until he can take them on an expensive adventure; eating more fruit and vegetables instead of waiting until he can afford expensive health food.... etc.) then he will be A) getting rid of the reason to have "lack of finances" as an excuse, and B) opening up and ALLOWING the money that is literally sitting there waiting to come to him. ;)

It also (of course) made me look at myself ;) - what we notice in others is a reflection of what's in ourselves - and I looked for where I was doing something similar.... and there it was, staring me in the face lol ☺

I have been (for years!) planning to clear out clutter in my house - and I've been waiting for changes in my life before I then clear it out (a move, money etc.) - to motivate me, to give me a reason to do it ... and I realized that if those changes were to occur now, having to then clear the clutter would hold me back on everything I'd want, and need, to do in those scenarios! So, two points:

1. I know that "acting as if" is very Powerful. So if I suddenly found out, without a doubt that I was definitely getting what I want, I'd be clearing that clutter like mad in preparation for it... and THEN it will happen automatically ;) And that is what gives the motivation and inspiration for clearing the clutter - acting "as if"

2. If I clear the clutter now, I'm breaking the spell of retaining the status quo - I'm getting rid of any pattern of keeping things as they are any reason that may be lurking for keeping the excuse of waiting for something to happen before doing what I need to do. ;)

I hope this helps others too. I'm very excited about it, and I'm off to do some more clutter-clearing now ;)

≪ ≪ ≪ ≫ ≫ ≫

Why do some people struggle and others don't?

I was asked this question this morning - what about people who are born into struggle with no hope of getting out of it - in certain countries, circumstances, and even some of us on this forum. It was a good question, and here's my take on it....

(I may be wrong of course, but this is what makes the most sense to me, and since none of us will know for certain the complete truth until we check out and look from the outside of this reality, all we can do is adopt the beliefs that make the most sense to us J)

If you think of life as the ultimate virtual reality game - "All that is" which is the massive energy power that is beyond our conscious understanding, but could be described as an infinite force of Energy – to some it's known as God, to some: The Universe -(our closest understanding to what that Power is, is the feeling of Unconditional Love)

That power projects itself into a physical "reality" - which gives the illusion of separateness, as well as everything we experience in this consciousness. Just like a virtual reality game - but it's particularly effective because it feels so real and has the added feature of total immersion - forgetting the true "reality" - a fully submersive virtual reality game)..... if that's the case, then it's possible that those people are the parts of that Power that have chosen to play the game on the "difficult" level this time round.

There's a computer game called "Heroes of Might and Magic" - and when you play the game on "Easy", you get an abundance of resources, you're surrounded by mines so you can mine more gold, coal, jewels etc. easily, the baddies aren't very tough, and generally it's not too much of a challenge....

But after you've played it like that a few times, you get bored because it's so easy.... so you play up a level - on that level, you start with fewer resources, mines are more difficult to find, and the opponents are a bit tougher, and there are more challenges and surprise attacks.....

Once you've played that a few times and managed to win it.... then you begin to want to challenge yourself more, because you believe you can do even better - the natural desire to achieve more.... so you move up to the next level.... and so on...

The most difficult level (I've never played it, but I know someone who has, and he really enjoyed the challenge and it took him many times of playing it to finally crack it) - you start with NO resources, it takes you foreeeeeeever to find the mines to get resources and gold, it's practically impossible to do anything without getting attacked by opponents (who, by the way, have PLENTY of resources!) .... and so you keep getting killed and having to start again....

However....

The All-Important difference is.... When playing that game you REMEMBER the progress from Easy upwards - you are fully conscious all the time from one level to the next, so when it gets difficult and seems impossible you remember that you chose this level and why.....

In this physical human game, of course, because it's a fully-submersive virtual reality game, we can't remember choosing this level, or why - or even that it's a game!

So, maybe, at times, it's an idea to bear in mind that it's a game - a strategy game that we've chosen to play at this level this time, and assume we've already played and conquered the easier levels and therefore we can get into the spirit of finding ways to win the game on this more difficult level....

Of course, we won't know the absolute truth until we "log out", but I feel it certainly helps to think this way in the meantime, even if it's not the truth (although I really believe it's pretty close to it ;)) ... it makes life less stressful in the meantime.

≪ ≪ ≪ ≫ ≫ ≫

An Interesting Perspective .....

Here's an analogy which helps to describe a possible explanation for why some people have such tough lives regardless of what they consciously do, and others seem to have it so easy.

Many people love to go to horror movies. I've always wondered why on earth people would deliberately cause themselves fear and terror and stress by watching these films... and it's still curious to me... but they are clearly choosing to voluntarily expose themselves to that experience... see where I'm going with this? Now, of course a person might say, but they are consciously CHOOSING to see the movie, whereas those who are struggling so much in life are not consciously choosing that experience .... which is true – but when people consciously choose to watch a horror movie, their body doesn't know about it. The body goes into survival mode just as if the threat is real. Palms get sweaty, adrenaline is released, heart-rate increases....

You could look at the physical experience ("life") as a movie theatre. Before entering this movie theatre complex, some choose drama, some choose romantic comedy, some choose horror, some choose thriller, some choose "rags to riches" (or "riches to rags"), some tragedy... and so on. And of course some genres are a mixture. Now, one could try and haul those people out of the horror movie theatre, to "save" them from the experience - and if one did, their bodies would be grateful Their bodies would experience relief and return to "normal"... but the person themselves would probably not be impressed. They would probably resist ;)

When I posted the above on a forum, the responses were all about how horror movies affect people, and explanations from readers detailing why they like to watch horror movies. Of course, this wasn't the point I was making – the horror movie was an analogy, but it's clearly quite a hot topic too! So, here's some clarification on why I used the analogy and how it relates to what I believe is the nature of "reality"...

Although it may be unfathomable to some of us why people choose to watch horror movies, they get something from it (and there are infinite reasons) - and there are many people who find sitting through a romantic comedy excruciating, and can't understand why someone would put themselves through that experience.....

And the point I was making is that we, as conscious beings make the decision to experience something for whatever reasons.... but our bodies don't have all the information and so they react as if the threat is REAL. In this analogy, the conscious part of us represents the "Higher Self" or whatever you call the greater, spiritual part of you... and the body represents our conscious awareness. It may sound a bit confusing... I'll put it simplistically just for the sake of clarity - it's obviously not this simplistic, but it'll help me explain it better: Imagine this world as a giant movie theatre complex. The Higher Self - the Greater part of us - has projected part of itself into this movie theatre complex to experience certain movies. The conscious part of us - the personality/ego/human - is in fact "unconscious" and reacts (as our bodies do during a horror movie) as if the threat is real.

And so... some people choose drama, some choose rags-to-riches, some choose riches-to-rags, some choose comedy, some choose horror, some choose feel-good, some choose adventure... and so on.... and each one is "living" the experience they've chosen - although the "body" (conscious part of them) has no idea it's a choice, and is reacting as if it's "real".

Meditation (and other forms of enlightenment) can be a way of reminding yourself "It's only a movie" ;)

Someone very close to me has been struggling in extremely difficult circumstances, and believes in his reasons for what he is doing. From my perspective, what he's "fighting against" is immovable... but he believes in it, and so he continues to suffer for what he believes to be the greater good. After much trying to help and to change his mind - or to help him to see from a different perspective, and trying to get him to choose an easier path - I had to finally accept that it is his choice, and that this is the experience he's chosen this time round. This is the way he's chosen to play the game this time round. And so, no matter how much I love him and want him to be safe and happy, and although I wouldn't choose to watch that movie myself, I have to accept and respect his choice of movie - it is the experience he wanted this time, even though his conscious part - the human (the "body") - has no idea it's only a movie ;)

And so, my intention in sharing this analogy was to help bring some peace to people in a similar situation - who may be feeling frustrated, helpless and/or stressed, watching a loved one live through something and making choices that seem beyond understanding - the analogy of movie choices can help to bring some clarity.

I believe that the physical experience is all about choice - whether it was the choice you made when you bought the ticket to come in, or whether it's the choice to change movie theatres during the movie ;)

« « « » » »

Getting Past Stubborn Negative Beliefs

I've had people ask me before how to deal with beliefs that are so engrained, that seem so real that they have trouble accepting anything new.

Whatever our subconscious is doing (and subconscious beliefs take time and experimenting to change since none of us really knows the cause of any specific subconscious belief - I once knew a man who was terrified of bananas and had no idea why) we DO have control over our conscious thoughts and decisions. And we make a choice to either continue on the same path, or to change at least our conscious thoughts.

An Elephant Never Forgets

Have you ever seen an elephant, staked at a circus ground? Have you ever wondered how that stake holds such a huge, strong animal? Did you know that often, when it's time to move on, the handler tells the elephant to pull the stake, and the animal uses its trunk to pull the stake out of the ground itself!

So, why doesn't the elephant just pull the stake out any old time he wants to go for a wander?

Because he's been taught that he can't - except for when the handler instructs him to. Isn't that Amazing, looking from our perspective? An animal that big, and that strong, is PHYSICALLY held in place - by a BELIEF!

Now, we, on the outside of that elephant's experience, can see the Truth. The truth is that the elephant is perfectly capable of setting himself free whenever he wants to. But from inside his perspective, he doesn't know that. And his belief is that he is chained and unable to wander off.

If the elephant could speak and reason, he would insist that he has no choice. He would insist that he is unable to walk away. If we said to him, but you can just pull the stake out with your trunk, he would answer "I can't! I can't do that! My whole life this stake has held me here. I believe in this stake, I mean look - it's there! It's in the ground, and my foot is chained to it. You can see it with your own eyes. The handler used a hammer to knock it into the ground. It's obvious I can't just pull it out. It's always held me here!" and he would reason it out. He would defend that belief that he is trapped - because that is his reality.

Now, if the elephant was happy where he was, and his handler was kind to him, and he was well cared for, then we might just look at the situation, and find it interesting, and we wouldn't try and convince the elephant of what we know. And it wouldn't matter what the elephant believes because he's happy.

However....

If the elephant is unhappy, if he feels trapped, or if he is ill-treated, it would be very frustrating trying to convince him that he is capable of ending his suffering if he would only choose to change his belief.

The problem is: there is no way this elephant can know the truth - he's been programmed to believe in the stake. And why should he trust us?

Let's say, another elephant actually did set himself free. And he tries to explain this to the trapped elephant. He says "I did it - it's absolutely possible! The stake is not keeping you trapped, your belief in it is!"

But the trapped elephant says, "But no-one knows that for sure!" The free elephant says, "Hey, that's true, and we'll never know for sure until we become human and we put the stakes in ourselves, but what I do know, is that when I changed my belief in the stake, I pulled it out with my trunk, and now I'm free!"

Then the other elephant has a choice - to find a way to change his beliefs ... or to continue believing in the stake. But the key word here is CHOICE.

He either CHOOSES to change or he CHOOSES to remain the same. Either way he is making his own choice.

He may not know HOW to change his belief, but the minute he TRULY decides that he WILL change his belief.... all manner of information and tools will come his way.

Maybe he starts to notice things he didn't before - like the fact that when his handler instructs him to pull the stake out of the ground to go to the water ... he may now become aware of how he does it, whereas before it was automatic. He may notice that when it's been raining and the ground is wet, the stake practically pulls itself out! He may begin to notice that his handler is too weak to push the broken down truck, and gets the elephant to do it - and this time, because of his awareness, he may begin to get a better idea of his own strength.... and so on.

Once he's chosen to change his beliefs, he begins to become open and to notice more.

But if he makes the CHOICE to continue with his current belief just because he believes it at the moment, and because even though he hates his life, the belief makes sense to him... then he will be living in that perspective and he'll never become aware of all the bits of information that make the NEW belief make more sense.

Every single moment of human consciousness is a choice. You can start making the choices that make you feel good! ☺

≪ ≪ ≪ ≫ ≫ ≫

A Very Simple Way to Keep Positive

I've found one simple thought to think which helps in feeling positive and loving towards whatever is in your life, which of course in turn helps you to attract what you do want.

We know that in order to attract what we want we need to be feeling good.

We also know that when we're feeling bad about what is, we're attracting more of that.

<u>Here's the simple thought that can help</u>:

"What's happening right now is a result of my previous actions and thoughts, but right now, in this moment, I'm creating new ones."

It's not so much to say that actual sentence, it's more to grasp the idea of it - literally just a thought.

<u>Here's the analogy</u> - you knew there had to be one with me! ;)

You found a pack of seeds and you were led to believe they're for red and yellow flowers, so you sprinkle them throughout your garden. But over time, as they start to show one by one, you find that they're a variety of ugly dark weeds.

Then someone gives you the right seeds for the pretty red and yellow flowers, and so you start sprinkling them throughout your garden. You've been told they're stronger than the weeds, and will grow regardless of the weeds.

However, after a day or two, you still see only weeds. This is because many of the weeds you sowed before haven't yet finished growing, some are slower than others, so they're still popping up. And of course, the seeds of the flowers are still busy growing roots - they won't show until they've grown a certain amount and start to show above the ground - and even then, you won't see the flowers for a while, they need time to reach the flowering stage. Over time you'll start seeing the red and yellow flowers you sowed popping up one by one in between the weeds.

So when you see a new weed, you can remind yourself that it's from the seeds you sowed before, and that you're now sowing the flower seeds each day; so soon, as long as you don't sow any more weed seeds, and you continue sowing flower seeds, eventually all the weeds will have grown and died off, and you'll be left with a garden full of flowers. ☺

It's very tempting to try and pull the weeds out or use weed-killer.... but the only way to end up with a garden full of flowers is to focus on sowing more flower seeds, and on nurturing the flowers that are there already.... and accept that the weeds will run their course and die out.

... and sometimes you'll sow weed seeds without realizing it until they start to show, but of course it will only be the odd one here and there because you'll be much more aware of what the flower seeds look like ;)

.... and sometimes (actually, often) there will be plants that look like weeds... which, if showered with unconditional love, will turn out to be just very special flowers once they are in full bloom. ;)

≪ ≪ ≪ ≫ ≫ ≫

Dealing with Doubts and Worries

A perspective that can help you to stop doubting

If (like most of us) you find that, despite changing your way of thinking – focusing on feeling good, keeping your thinking positive, and changing your beliefs – you're still not seeing the results you want, there may be times you feel despondent and doubtful. Here's an analogy that may help:

When you plant a seed, you expect it to take some time before you start to see the plant above the ground. And so you **water the spot each day** and **you get on with life while you wait for it to appear.**

You don't keep digging it up to see why it's not showing above the ground yet. ;)

Your **desire is the seed** you've planted. And **the good stuff you do for yourself and your positive attitude, following what feels good etc - that's watering it**. Make sure you do that **each day.**

But **every time you doubt, and analyze, and worry** - that's like **digging up the seed** wondering why it's not growing. And of course, each time you dig up the seed to have a look and worry, **you're delaying its growth** - you might even eventually kill it because it just doesn't have time to take root.

Remind yourself every time you start to feel doubt: "I'm digging up the seed again! I'm going to leave it alone now, water it by following what feels good, and allow it to grow. When it's ready (in its own good time) I will see it start to appear above the ground. In the meantime, there's no point sitting watching the ground and waaaaaiting for it... I'll get on with the rest of my life while it's busy growing beneath the surface." ☺

≪ ≪ ≪ ≫ ≫ ≫

Dealing With Doubts and Worries Q & A

Q: two thoughts come to my mind:

1. What if the seed I planted is dead? How do you reconcile that? The only way you will know if it is dead or not is by digging the hole up and looking at it. And that would surely prevent it from sprouting if it were alive. Man, this is such a catch 22!!

2. Sometimes, despite all your effort, the seed still doesn't sprout because it may be damaged or the conditions in the terrain changed. I struggle with doubt, not about my desire but about its fruition because I do not see ANY tangible effects or movement towards it.

A: Good questions! 1. You know if your seed is dead or not by how you feel. If you feel excited by it, if it makes you feel good - that's your indication it is very much alive and perfectly capable of growing. In fact the moment you want it, it starts growing. So as long as it feels good, it's growing.

2. The only thing your seed needs is unconditional love *(see the chapter: "You Have a Superpower")*. That's all it needs. As long as you're giving it that, it can't help but grow, it's just that it may take a while before you see the results "above ground". And you know you're giving it unconditional love - again by how you feel. And the best way to "water" your seed with unconditional love is to focus on other things - other things that make you feel good.

Follow what feels good in the moment - like a treasure trail - even if it doesn't appear to have anything to do with your seed. Sometimes we're led to our desires by the most bizarre detours ;) As long as you are following what genuinely feels good in the moment, you are moving towards your desire and your seed is growing. You will see the results when it breaks the surface of the earth ;)

Q: i have a question. What if you know that the reasons your plant is growing so slow or not at all is because there are "diseases" (i.e. limiting beliefs) in the root of the plant or in the ground. everytime you plant a new plant, it never grows or grows slowly and eventually dies. how do you get rid of that "disease" that keeps killing what you plant?

A: Good question - and this is a very real issue. We definitely have control over our conscious beliefs - we can choose in the moment (even though sometimes it doesn't feel like we have a choice) what to think and feel; however, subconscious patterns and beliefs we're generally not even aware of never mind able to control.

There are many, many tools that help access and change subconscious beliefs - from psychological to spiritual - and it's a case of finding the tool that works for you. Many tools work for some people and not for others - and adjusting the conscious mind's perspective (like the example of the seeds in this thread) can help maximize the effects of whatever tools you do use to change subconscious programming.

So, of course, it's important to find the right tool (or combination of tools) for you to heal those "diseases", and while you're treating your soil with those, keep reminding yourself that it takes time for plants to grow, even in the healthiest soil. ;)

≪ ≪ ≪ ≫ ≫ ≫

The Dog Whisperer Method of Changing Thought Patterns

I wanted to share some insight that has come to me while watching the TV program "The Dog Whisperer", which I believe can be very helpful for retraining the mind to more positive thoughts...

In "The Dog Whisperer", Cesar Millan rehabilitates dogs from some of the most dramatic issues. And one of the main reasons it works so effectively and so quickly, is that dogs live in the moment. Since they don't reason, when they are being rehabilitated, they don't think "This isn't going to work - I've tried this before!" or "This is ridiculous - I've tried Everything!" and so on. They just follow the lead .... and the brain Automatically makes new associations. And it's like Magic.

There are three main requirements that Cesar introduces:

1. Exercise

2. Rules, boundaries, limitations

3. Affection

And in that order. The reason for putting exercise first, is that the brain is less open to learning or paying attention when there is pent up energy.

So, how does it apply to us? ....

1. Exercise:

When we have subconscious programming that results in negative habitual thinking, it generally builds up a lot of negative energy, frustration, anger, fear and so on. Before we're able to be receptive to a new, more positive and calm way of thinking, we need to drain that negative energy. Just as Cesar advises draining the pent up energy in the dog by giving him enough exercise before attempting to make any changes... so we sometimes need to find a way to drain the pent up negative energy before we're able to be fully open and receptive to changing our habitual thinking.

We can do this through physical activity - running, sport, punching pillows, screaming therapy, dancing etc. and/or through expressing it in writing. Write a letter you'll never send. It can be a general open letter to everyone; or a letter to one or more people in particular.

In this letter, write absolutely everything that comes into your mind. Insult, cuss, blame, rant, rave, be unreasonable - just get it all out and onto the page/screen. Once you've drained that negative energy, your mind will be more receptive and open to new thought patterns and habits - more positive ones.

2. Rules, boundaries, limitations:

The way Cesar corrects a dog when it displays unwanted behavior, is by making a short, sharp "ch" sound. This snaps the dog out of the unwanted state of mind, and into an attentive state. This is usually required several times before the change becomes natural.

He teaches that timing is the key - to catch the intention **before it escalates**. This requires becoming **aware** of the dog's change in attitude, and correcting at the **very first sign**. This way, the behavior doesn't escalate.

So, for ourselves, if we become aware of our thoughts, we can catch ourselves at the first sign, and correct our habitual thinking immediately - nipping it in the bud with a short, sharp "ch" ;) Well, of course it doesn't have to be a "ch" but I find that's very effective - especially after watching "The Dog Whisperer" because my mind is used to hearing it as a correction. But you can have a word or another sound. And of course, the sound doesn't have to be out loud, you can say it in your head. It's a way of snapping your automatic thinking out of that frame of mind in the moment, **before it takes hold.**

3. Affection:

Of course, this is something most of us are lacking when it comes to displaying it to ourselves. Find ways to show yourself affection. Do **at least one thing** for yourself **each day**, just because it feels good. Do for yourself what you wish someone else would do for you. Treat yourself the same way you treat loved ones - with the same compassion and the same consideration.

And finally, Cesar teaches that the most important ingredient to being successful is a **Calm, Assertive energy**. This works with dogs of course - BUT it ALSO works with humans - AND with ourselves!! Practicing being in a Calm Assertive state does wonders for your vibration, your state of mind, and helps to build a feeling of reassurance and confidence within yourself. On top of that, you'll notice a marked change in how others respond to you when you're in that state.

I HIGHLY recommend watching "The Dog Whisperer" even if you don't have dogs (I don't have a dog, but I'm intrigued by the process) - and while you're watching, see how much you can relate the issues and processes to the subconscious mind, your own issues, and your own rehabilitation. ☺

≪ ≪ ≪ ≫ ≫ ≫

Respect, Self Esteem and The Dog Whisperer!

Many people feel they can only gain respect by intimidation (others by manipulation) because they don't realize there is any other way. Like everything else, it's based in self esteem.

People who use intimidation or manipulation to get respect, loyalty or obedience have a basic **subconscious belief** that they **don't deserve** or are **not entitled** to respect, loyalty or obedience automatically. Therefore, they assume there's **no way the other person is simply going to give it to them** - so they have to find a way to **take it!**

In the TV program: **"The Dog Whisperer"** the **most Valuable lesson**, which applies to human relationships as well as dogs, is the energy of **"Calm-Assertive".**

Anyone who wants to gain respect - and this is especially important of course for **parents, teachers, bosses**, and anyone else whose job depends on retaining respect and authority - needs to learn to adopt this "Calm-Assertive" energy.

A calm-assertive energy **compels** people to VOLUNTARILY GIVE respect and loyalty, whereas bullying, demanding, intimidating and threatening tries to TAKE respect and loyalty. And of course, what they get instead of respect and loyalty is fear and resentment

It's like going into a **bank** and **holding up the cashier** to take out your own money! :D If you fill in the withdrawal slip, and ask for your money, the cashier will happily hand it over. But a person who doesn't know that, and **believes** that they're **not entitled to their money**, may well believe that since they're not good enough, there's no way anyone will just give it to them if they ask ... they may well believe the **only way** to get it is to **force** the cashier to hand it over!

Calm-Assertive. It's really worth watching Cesar Millan in "The Dog Whisperer", and applying his energy to all human relationships.

«« «« «« »» »» »»

The LOA Treasure Hunt Trail to What You Want

Simply following what feels good in the moment is like following a treasure hunt trail to what you want.

Following what feels good in the moment is the shortest route, of least resistance, to what you want - even if it seems completely unrelated!!

Here's an example scenario:

Peter has a blue Ford Escort he wants to sell.

Sally needs a car, and she'd prefer a Ford Escort because she learned to drive in one. Since it's second-hand, she doesn't mind what color, but ideally, she'd like blue, if it's the right price.

Peter puts ads in the newspaper, and he puts a sign on the car, but no luck selling it yet. Then, he has a desire to go bowling one night. He just feels it would be fun to do. On his way to the bowling alley, he feels hungry, and fancies a candy bar. So he stops off at the gas station on the way.

Meanwhile, Sally's friend has called her to go and see a movie. Sally's not sure she should go as she's pouring through the newspapers, looking for a car. She needs to get one really soon, and she's getting desperate, but the cars she's found for sale in her area are all out of her price range. She's tempted to stay in and continue looking through the papers and online... but she knows it would feel so good to go to a movie with her friend... so eventually she "gives in" and accepts. Her friend picks her up, and they drive to the cinema. On the way, her friend realizes she needs to draw cash, so she pulls into the gas station where they have a cash machine.

Sally's friend asks if she'd like to go in with her, or wait in the car. Sally doesn't feel like getting out - she feels comfortable and cozy in the car, so she chooses to wait there.

While she's sitting waiting for her friend, Peter pulls up next to her, to get his chocolate bar... and she notices the sign in the window of his car - it's for sale, it's a Ford Escort, it's blue... and the price is perfect. Sally gets out of her friend's car, speaks to Peter, they switch numbers and call it a coincidence. ;)

THAT is how I believe the LOA works. Follow the breadcrumb trail of what feels good in the moment (no matter how unrelated it may seem) to what you want.

≪ ≪ ≪ ≫ ≫ ≫

A Tale of Two Countries

You Don't Need to Get What You Want to be Happy, But You DO Need to be Happy to Get What You Want ;)

There are two countries. Most of us live in Whatis.... and all the stuff we want resides in Happiness. The stuff we want can't leave Happiness because if it did, it would change form and become the same as the rest of the stuff in Whatis. Happiness is what makes the stuff what it is. So we have to travel to Happiness to get the stuff in person.

There are many, many roads between the two countries - all of them one-ways, but there are two main highways leading from Whatis to Happiness, and they are called Unconditional Love and the Happiness Highway itself. Both of these lead directly to Happiness, from Whatis, and are the fastest routes there, but there are many minor roads which also lead there, indirectly, along the scenic routes.

Now, because most people have no idea that all the stuff they've ordered and created is located in Happiness, they spend most of their time searching through Whatis for it. And they often end up getting terribly lost, wandering around the maze of roads. Roads like Worry Crescent, Frustration Way, Impatience Drive, Angry Walk, Depression Avenue, and the many others like them. And when they're not in that maze of roads, they're drifting through Bland Valley without even realizing it.

But no matter how long they spend searching through Whatis, no matter how many roads they go down, no matter how determined they are, as long as they stay in Whatis, of course, they're never going to get to their stuff - because it's not there, it's in a completely different country.

And sometimes, people get fed up, and so they sit on the side of the road and wait for their stuff to come to them. But it can't. If it leaves Happiness, it's different stuff.

And everyone has been given the impression that in fact they CAN'T get to Happiness on their own. They can't just go there. They have to wait for their stuff and their stuff will take them there. But the truth is: their stuff is already there. And not only are they ABLE to go there on their own, but it's the ONLY WAY to move there. ;)

Sometimes, in their wanderings, people find themselves on one of the roads to Happiness - sometimes it's one of the main highways, many times it's one of the minor routes.. sometimes it's by accident, sometimes it's on purpose. But because they don't realize that's the ONLY place to find their stuff, they usually turn off onto one of the one-ways leading back to Whatis when they see the signs to Whatis - even though the signs are pointing in the opposite direction to where they want to go. And so they end up on one of the roads leading back to Whatis, like the Disappointment Freeway.

And so they keep ending up back in Whatis. But, once they find out that while they stay in Whatis, they'll never get their stuff because it won't - can't - ever come to them in Whatis, that they have to move to Happiness to get it (they're bound to visit Whatis sometimes of course - vacations and so on ;)) - THEN they can find the route they prefer, and make the move. And they also then know that when they accidently follow the signs that lead back to Whatis, they can turn around and get back on the right road again, leading towards Happiness, where their stuff waits for them.

And once they make the move to Happiness, then at least they're in the right country, and then, while they wander around, sight-seeing in that beautiful place - Fun Alley, Easy Street, the shores of the Fanta Sea, and the peaks of Mt. Laughter, and all the other wonderful experiences Happiness provides - while they're doing that, they're in the right country for THEIR STUFF to FIND THEM! ;)

《 《 《 》 》 》

The Truth About Feeling Sorry for Yourself

Most of us (as far as I know) are raised with the belief that it is selfish and "wrong" to "feel sorry for yourself" - we're programmed with "Stop feeling sorry for yourself..." - and the idea of feeling sorry for yourself becomes confused and enmeshed with "wallowing" and negativity, but there is a Very Important difference....

As we know, our feelings are our Guidance System.

When experiencing hurt, anger, frustration, sorrow, depression, disappointment....etc. there is a natural urge which leads towards healing. If we were to "go with the flow" on feelings alone, most of us would probably feel really sorry for ourselves for a while, comfort ourselves, and then find ways to feel better, and eventually get back into the game.

A person who has been programmed against "feeling sorry for myself" will generally fight the natural urge to be compassionate with themselves, and will probably treat themselves in the same way as(and sometimes worse than) they were treated by whoever taught them this belief. Many others who have been programmed with this belief will rebel against it despite the belief.... and this comes out in complaining, and seeking sympathy from others. It can also fester and become aggression, resentment... and of course a variety of other symptoms.

That person will take much longer to heal (if they heal at all) than someone who feels sorry for themselves until they feel better.

There is a fear that feeling sorry for yourself is quicksand and that once you step into that mode you're not going to come out of it again. But that is called despondency, not "feeling sorry for yourself". And if you do a good job of feeling sorry for yourself (as described below) despondency is not on the menu!

If someone you love is physically hurt, it's highly unlikely you'd have no sympathy or compassion for them and that you'd push them and force them to keep going and ignore their cries of pain. You'd probably look after them, treat them kindly and compassionately, encourage them to rest, maybe even spoil them a little, and do what you could to make them feel better and to speed up their healing.

And yet we usually don't treat our own emotional, mental and spiritual pain and healing in the same way.

These are the fastest, most effective steps to aid healing (physical, emotional, mental and spiritual):

1. Feel sorry for yourself - meaning a combination of **Compassion and Acknowledgment**.

2. Treat yourself as you would a loved one who is recovering from surgery.

3. Do whatever feels good in the moment, no matter how "self indulgent" - it is part of your treatment and it will **speed up your healing**.

4. **Follow what feels good in the moment**. If you follow what feels good in the moment, you will come through the self pity, move into self comforting, move on to indulgence, and then to inspiration and finally back to action. And it's important to let each stage play through fully until you naturally and automatically find yourself in the next one. As

long as you're following what feels good in the moment, you can't go wrong, and you will not stay in any one state indefinitely.

I came across a few sites entitled "How to stop feeling sorry for yourself" - I have to admit, I didn't explore every one of them, but those I did visit all detailed ways of avoiding feeling sorry for yourself

In my opinion (and experience) the most effective way to stop feeling sorry for yourself, is to ALLOW yourself to feel sorry for yourself ;) Denying it and avoiding it only sends subconscious messages that you have no right to compassion and acknowledgement, that you are not worthy, that your feelings are invalid... which can lead to self-sabotage, beliefs of undeserving... and a host of other destructive programming

Allowing yourself a GOOD self-pity session is like comforting a child who has scraped his knee, enabling him to get the acknowledgement, validation and reassurance he needs in order for him to get over it and get on with the rest of the activity (resulting in his realizing for HIMSELF that it isn't that bad ;)) - instead of telling him he'll live and it's not like he lost a leg.

So, go ahead and feel sorry for yourself! Give yourself permission. It's giving your self a soft place to fall before you rest, recover and get up again.

Feeling Sorry for Yourself Q & A

I've had some questions, queries and objections from people, which I thought I'd share here, with my answers to them:

Q: "What if the thing that you use to 'indulge yourself' is what is hurting you? Like an addiction?"

A: Good point! I'm no expert on addiction, but I have a little experience of it, and from my limited knowledge, I think that the "good" feeling from giving in to an addiction, is not the same as the feeling you might get from doing something that feels good but that you're not addicted to.

For example, if a person is addicted to gambling, the feeling they get when gambling may feel good, but it will also be mixed with a variety of other feelings - possibly guilt, danger, fear, desperation... it won't feel the same as, for example, riding a skate-board (if that feels good obviously) or playing a Wii game they enjoy, or having a bubble bath... or ... whatever else makes them feel good - there will be a distinct difference in feeling between the addictive behavior, and behavior that just feels good - without the baggage that goes with addiction.

So, following what feels good means following what makes you feel good without any of those extra feelings. Indulging in what feels good, without strings attached.

If a person has an addiction, then obviously the idea would be to indulge in things that they're not addicted to. If they have an alcohol addiction, then indulging in bubble baths, computer games, chocolate, watching movies, starting a new activity, martial arts.... or whatever else feels genuinely good at the time, would be more effective. Of course, if they indulge in their addiction, they're creating more negativity for themselves. So, finding other ways to pamper and comfort themselves would be more effective.

Q: *(This one is edited due to strong language)*

All I need to do is remind myself of conditions in sweatshops that nike, adidas, walmart, old navy, gap, that employ millions of third world country inhabitants and I quickly stop feeling sorry for myself. These corporations have children working 12 hour days, 6 day weeks, with 2 breaks. If a kid tries to take an extra break, they get beaten. They live in 9x9 foot cement cells and eat rice with salt 2 meals a day. ...Many families make a choice between them or their children eating every day. If you tip over a carosine lamp, you probably won't be eating for 3 days because something so small would create a huge financial tragedy.

So if I get rejected by a girl that I ask on a date, score a bad mark on a test, or my parents "yell" at me... Guess what? I don't feel sorry for myself. You, and everyone else that made a post on this thread has no **** reason to feel sorry for yourself ever.

A: I understand what you're saying because it's the viewpoint most of us are raised with, which is why I wrote this post. ;)

Your not feeling sorry for yourself doesn't help those children in any way at all. What it does do however, is reinforce low self esteem and self worth in you. I suspect you're not going to accept that - I may be wrong of course ;) - because I get the impression from your post that you're very passionate about your belief that those who aren't suffering as much as others have nothing to complain about. And this is very strong programming in a lot of us, so I'm not trying to convince you to agree, just explaining what I meant about feeling sorry for yourself.

If, in being tough on himself, a person was thereby making the smallest improvement to the experience of even just one of those children you mentioned, then I would be writing a very different post!

The way you treat yourself has no effect on the millions of people suffering in the world. For that, there are causes and organizations to donate to, volunteer for, and even start up from scratch.... the way you treat yourself only has an effect on your own beliefs, your own self esteem, self worth, feelings of deserving and behavior... and in turn, of course, on the people around you.

"Stop feeling sorry for yourself, there are others much worse off than you!" was a tool introduced by parents who didn't know how else to handle their children. They used that "logic" because it was the only way they could think of to make their child "snap out of it and get on with it". They didn't realize that showing the child compassion and acknowledgement is the fastest, most effective way to help them to "snap out of it and get on with it". Because the child has received acknowledgement and compassion, he's able to let go and move on.

But if he's given the message he has no right to feelings of compassion and sympathy, and his feelings are not acknowledged - by being told to "Stop feeling sorry for yourself, there are others worse off than you.." the message being programmed into his subconscious is that he has no right to express his feelings... which can result in suppressed feelings...

which can result in subconscious resentment, rage and any number of other things... which then come out in a variety of ways. And these are seen to be issues in themselves, instead of symptoms of programming - the basis of which is: "I don't matter."

And this "logic" which is based in low self esteem and low self worth of "You have no right to complain when there are so many others so much worse off than you." has been carried down from generation to generation, like many other things, and because it's been programmed into them as children, those who keep that belief, program it into their own children ... and so the legacy of low self esteem, low self worth, and beliefs of undeserving continues...

Showing compassion and acknowledgement to yourself, in the same way you would show it for someone else you care about, can only have a positive effect on you and those around you - if, as I said, you do it right ;)

Q: hmm..I don't agree. but its your wording I don't agree with mostly.

feeling sorry for yourself doesn't mean you heal

feeling sorry for yourself doesn't mean you overcome a problem

feeling sorry for yourself, just means that, you feel sorry yourself. it is an end to itself and a way to continually make excuses to feel sorry for yourself. solutions don't magically appear in thin air when you feel sorry for yourself. rather, you see more things to feel sorry about. that's why it's an end to itself. when you feel sorry for yourself, the sky's the limit of what else to feel sorry about!

**there are a lot of people who feel constantly sorry for themselves
1. some are shallow**

2. others are really suffering and have probably been suffering their whole lives, born into poverty, disease, so on

3. others are suffering from a mental disease, like depression that makes them feel sorry for themselves, when there might not be any reason to be

words are symbolic, they have no definitive meaning, but the meaning we give to them

I feel you are changing the meaning of feeling sorry for yourself to "letting out your emotions"

letting out your emotions is important, like you said, your emotional guidance system. if you need to cry. cry. if you need to be angry. be angry. emotions however are normally INSTANT. and for a lot of times, even more so with depression, they feel uncontrollable. like laughing. how many people can genuinely force themselves to laugh? a lot of people can't.

thoughts however are controllable unless you are clinically insane. for us sane people, we can control our thoughts.

Thats the difference between thoughts and emotions. feeling sorry for yourself is a mental action. not an emotional action. feeling sorry for yourself are THOUGHTS.

1. "my car is crappy"

2. "my job sucks"

3. "my friends suck"

4. "I'm fat"

5. "I'm ugly"

6. "I'm a loser"

7. "I hate my life yatta yatta yatta"

do you understand?

these are thoughts WE CONTROL. they are not emotions.

rather negative thoughts GENERATE negative emotions that make us feel really crappy

if you understand the concept of the emotional guidance system, the idea is, your emotions are your ultimate guide to what is 'good' and what is 'bad'. to what makes you happy, and what makes you miserable. if something makes you feel crappy, its a 'bad'. thinking negative thoughts like "I hate myself" makes you feel CRAPPY. You emotional guidance system is telling you these thoughts are BAD. Stop thinking them!! THESE THOUGHTS MAKE YOU MISERABLE. They are NOT healing you. Thats how you use the emotional guidance system with thoughts. Pay attention to how thoughts make you feel.

This is also the LOA. Your emotional guidance system will ALWAYS let you know the quality of your thoughts.

And if you feel 'good' when you hate yourself or your life, thats usually a sure sign you are not mentally/emotionally healthy and might need professional help before you start physically harming yourself

Like I said, feeling sorry for yourself will never heal you. It will never solve your problems. And it usually BLINDS you from solutions.

The poor man can feel sorry for himself every day because he's a mr. empty pockets - money will never magically manifest because he's miserable.

The girl who was just dumped can feel sorry for herself in every social event she goes to. Her bad vibes and jealousy won't attract a new relationship into her life, or help her get over the past.

If cry then cry. You are emotionally distraught. Be emotionally distraught. The death of a loved one is literally for most of us, unimaginable.

But thinking negative thoughts? It will never do you any good.

If the poor man feels sorry for himself and says "I might as will give up, I'll always be poor!". Then he lacks the motivation and the self confidence needed to achieve abundance in his life.

Self defeating ego thoughts. That is what feeling sorry for yourself really means. Thats why feeling sorry for yourself has always been frowned on. It is NOT the same as expressing your emotions.

A: I think you may have misunderstood what I meant by "Feeling sorry for yourself". As I mentioned, what I'm referring to is Compassion + Acknowledgement - feeling (not thinking, feeling) the way for yourself that you would for someone else you care about.

Most of us are raised to be tough on ourselves, to treat ourselves harshly. When something happens that makes you feel bad, if you just force yourself to feel better - in other words, you force yourself to push away the "bad" feelings and feel better (and many people who are trying to work with the LOA do this), what you're doing is suppressing those "bad" feelings - and they will probably come out in some other way.

Quote:

"Thats the difference between thoughts and emotions feeling sorry for yourself is a mental action. not an emotional action. feeling sorry for yourself are THOUGHTS."

I disagree. Feeeeeeling sorry for yourself - is a feeeeeling "Thinking sorry for yourself" would be thoughts ;)

Quote:

"1. "my car is crappy"

2. "my job sucks"

3. "my friends suck"

4. "I'm fat"

5. "I'm ugly"

6. "I'm a loser"

7. "I hate my life yatta yatta yatta""

You're right, these are thoughts - but they're not "Feeling sorry for yourself" The thoughts may create negative feelings, but the thoughts are not what I'm referring to.

What I'm talking about is illustrated in this example:

If you get hurt by someone, and you begin to feel sad, and you tell yourself to snap out of it, and you force yourself to not feel sad, there's a message you're giving to yourself. If a friend you care about had the same experience, and they told you about it, you would (presumably) show them sympathy and compassion, and you would (presumably) acknowledge their feelings and what had happened.

The message getting programmed into your subconscious is that your friend's feelings are important and valid, but yours are not and you don't have a right to them.

Whereas, if you treat yourself the way you'd treat your friend - with the same sympathy, compassion and acknowledgement - like your friend, once you feel your feelings have been validated and acknowledged, you will then NATURALLY move up the emotional guidance scale.

Now, of course, if something happens to you and you feel hurt by it, if you're able to just let it go and move on – genuinely, not by forcing yourself or belittling your feelings – then obviously, that's great! ☺ What I'm referring to is when you can't do that, when the feelings are too strong and the hurt too deep, and there's a tendency to bully yourself into moving on. That's really what this is about. ☺

Hope this helps to clarify.

Q: I think that the words "sorry for yourself" are what people are having a problem with.

A: The reason I specifically use the words "Feeling sorry for yourself" is because they are usually used to criticize people for feeling compassion for themselves. ☺

When someone is hurting, and they're expressing that hurt, it's very common for them to be told (especially by parents) "Don't feel sorry for yourself" or "Stop feeling sorry for yourself" - this creates a feeling of shame around feeling compassion for oneself ... which in turn often results in the person being hard on themselves, and critical of themselves.... which is usually accompanied by an underlying, unconscious resentment.

Q: I recently discovered that I am a people pleaser. The problem is that I share a lot with my mother. I was discussing this with her and because of the boundless emotion associated with finally

realizing this about myself I started to cry. I knew it would pass because it was a release for me, as it always is. EVERYTIME I cry when talking to my mother she scolds me and tells me to stop. I am so tired of it that we end up in a fight over the fact that she has never let me just "be." I am never good enough for her

We ended up discussing the difference between feeling sorry for someone and compassion before I eventually hung up on her. She said they were not different. I said they were VERY different.

I believe that if you feel sorry for someone you take away their personal power. Compassion comes from a place of love and empathy. If I have compassion for someone without food I would teach them to fish not give them fish. If I felt sorry for someone I would just give them fish.

What do you think?

A: Good point! First of all, I suspect that the reason your mother tells you to stop crying, and the reason she's so insistent and volatile about it, is that she's uncomfortable with raw emotion. Many, many people become extremely uncomfortable when someone cries. One of the reasons for this is often because they feel helpless and vulnerable themselves. It brings up in them, emotions they don't know how to handle. So they only feel the impulse to make it stop. It's emotionally painful because they can't make it stop - this discomfort. They also often have core beliefs that if they tried to comfort the person, it would increase and encourage the crying. Ironically, it's a bit like not giving someone food when they're hungry because you believe that it will encourage them to want more food.

Very few people are comfortable with just allowing someone to cry, without needing them to stop. (Unconditional Love is the Power that truly and comfortably allows this) It's actually very freeing. In fact, when a child throws a tantrum - it's difficult when others are affected, for example in public, but when it happens in the privacy of your own home, it's freeing for both parent and child, to ALLOW the child to cry - without doing anything to try and stop them; without feeling any resistant energy. Just literally Allowing. Not allowing in a resentful or "giving up" kind of way, or with any negative emotion or attitude. Just allowing as you allow them to play or breath or sleep. With kindness and love.

There's not much you can say to your mum that would change this. It's something that is probably a core belief in her, and logic or debate won't change that. However.... what I do believe will Definitely make a difference, is using your Superpower (*see the chapter "You Have a Superpower*). I know that if you do that, and if you're prepared to accept that sometimes it takes a bit of practice - you will notice a difference! ☺

There is of course, as you've pointed out, a big difference between feeling sympathy, and feeling compassion. The example you give regarding the fish is a good one. ☺

Q: I thank you so much for everything you described about "feeling sorry for ones self". You proved to me and another friend that it is ok to feel this way and hearing the saying "Stop feeling sorry for yourself" demotivates a persons will to heal. I had a terrible argument today with my best friend who I feel less trust for than I ever used to. She Always says that stupid saying and tries to unjustify the way I feel and convinces me that I don't care about anyone but myself and that I am selfish when clearly I devote all of my attention towards her. What do I do?

A: I'm so glad the post helped.

As to what to do about your friend... It seems to me that your friend has major insecurity issues and probably core beliefs that she is unworthy and unlovable. Logic and debate is usually ineffective against core beliefs. The beliefs are so much part of the foundation of who the person is, that they over-ride all information or "evidence" to the contrary. The only way they can be changed is if the person themselves recognizes them as beliefs and not truth... and if they are determined to make the changes.

The phrase "Stop feeling sorry for yourself" carries powerful emotion and energy. It's full of fear and insecurity. And of course, it's a program, not an original thought. It's something that has been said to that person from childhood, which is then passed on... like "Money doesn't grow on trees" or "All good things must come to an end" or "You'll never get anywhere" or "Life is tough"... and so on. It's just a program, like a computer virus. But if the owner of the computer believes the program is part of the genuine hardware of the computer, they'll just keep using it and of course, they'll never get rid of it because they believe the computer wouldn't work without it.

It's only if the owner of the computer recognizes and acknowledges that it's not a real program, but a virus... only then will they be prepared to A) not open it deliberately, and B) find a way to clear their computer of it. ☺

But... using your Superpower (see the chapter "You Have a Superpower") will make changes you wouldn't believe! That is the one thing I can tell you will work - if you do it, and stick to it. I believe that if you do it as described, you'll see magical changes in your relationship with your friend! ☺

≪ ≪ ≪ ≫ ≫ ≫

If You Can't Stop Being Hard On Yourself

Imagine a horse that has been ill-treated. And the person who has just bought it wants it to pull a cart. So he hitches the half-starved, beaten and bleeding animal to the cart, and when the horse can't even move because it is so damaged, the new owner shouts at it, and beats it some more.... is that horse EVER likely to be able to pull that cart?

Now, if the new owner takes that horse to a vet, and then nurses it back to health with love, nourishment, compassion and caring. If he speaks to the horse with gentle and encouraging words, if he tells the horse it's going to be okay, it's going to get better; If he shows the horse he loves it; If he lets it rest in a comfortable stable where it's warm and safe; And if he allows it, as it gets better, to graze in the sunshine, and on the days it feels worse, if he gives it extra caring and love.... that horse will heal and get stronger, and it will then be ABLE and Willing to pull that cart!

You are that horse. The previous owners who ill-treated you are those who raised you. The NEW owner is YOU! It's up to YOU now to put down the whip, unhitch yourself from that cart, and give yourself some nursing back to health with Love and Compassion and Caring - or, just like the horse you won't be ABLE to heal. You can't heal while you're continuing to beat yourself emotionally, where your previous "carers" left off.

One of the first steps you can take in putting down the whip and unhitching yourself from the cart, and starting to help yourself heal, is to start doing things you love. Even if you start with just one. And at first it may feel odd. Even the horse would find it odd to be suddenly treated with kindness instead of being shouted at and beaten. He may well even react with suspicion. But with coaxing and reassurance from his new owner, he will slowly begin to accept and respond to the new experience of kindness.

Many of us find it difficult at first, to focus on doing what feels good, and it can be a challenge to show ourselves compassion and kindness.

Do something Delicious for yourself today! ☺

≪ ≪ ≪ ≫ ≫ ≫

If You Feel You Can't Stop Struggling

Those for whom this was written will recognize it ;)

It's like being in a room where you feel trapped, and you can see a window, and you're sure you could get through it, but it has bars on it. So you try to bend the bars but they won't budge.

So you look around on the floor, searching for something to help. Then you see a saw, and you're so excited - the saw must be for the bars. So you start working day and night, sawing at those bars, and you put everything into it, and you believe. And then the saw breaks. And you're devastated. And you're desperate to get out. You feel like you'll suffocate if you stay there any longer.

Then, someone outside the window tells you that what you need to do is to lie down on the bed and sleep. But you cannot see how that's going to help you get out of the room. Lying down on the bed is not going to bend those bars! Lying down on the bed is not going to break those bars, or make the window any bigger.

So you look around near the window again, looking for another way to get rid of these bars. And you try and figure out if there's something else you can do to bend them or break them.

And then, someone puts a crowbar through the window. And you're so grateful! So, you start trying to bend the bars with the crowbar. And again you work day and night, you put all your energy and focus into it and you work so hard. But the bars won't budge. The crowbar eventually bends but the bars stay solid.

And again, the person outside says that you need to rest and look after yourself. That is the only way to get out. Lie down on the bed and sleep. Of course, this still makes no sense. You'll sleep when you've got the job done. But you have to get these bars bent or broken before you suffocate in this room!

So you search the room, looking for something that will help to bend or break these bars. And you find a blow torch under the bed!! WOW!! Okay, now you're feeling positive and energized! Thank you SO much to whoever left this blow torch here. You see, there is always a way, and you trusted and believed, and you were rewarded. So you pick up the blow torch, and you go over to the window..... and the blow torch doesn't work. It's broken!

Devastation again. You could explode with frustration. Every time you try.... Everything you try... you just keep getting thwarted. What are you supposed to do! You've done Everything you can. You've worked SO hard. It's not like you're just sitting around waiting for someone to rescue you. You're doing Everything you can think of!

... and so it goes on.

And you remember the advice to lie down on the bed and sleep. But you still cannot see how it will help, and every day you get more desperate to get out - you can feel the suffocation creeping up on you - and every day that you get more desperate, it seems more and more ridiculous to just lie down on the bed and sleep!! There's no time to lie down on the bed - every moment resting is a moment that is wasted and it's another moment that could be spent on the bars. And anyway, how can you just relax and sleep when you're worried about how you're going to get out of that window? ....

Until one day, exhausted, you decide "FINE!! Okay. I'll lie down on the *%#*#* bed!!" ;)

And so you lie down on the bed. And you fall asleep. And your body and mind rest. And when you wake up, you open your eyes. And there, just above your head, is a switch. You've never seen it before because you've never laid down on the bed for long enough. You've been so preoccupied with the bars that even when you have laid down for a moment, you've been looking at the window, trying to figure out another way.

So you press the switch - and a light comes on. The light fills the room - you didn't even know there WAS a light in this room. And as you sit up on the bed. There, directly opposite the bed, the opposite side of the room to the window, is a door! And the door is ajar. ;)

Of course, you would never have dreamt that lying down on the bed would have been the answer to getting out of the room. It made absolutely no sense. Now, you realize that if you hadn't laid down on the bed and had a good long sleep, you wouldn't have woken refreshed enough to notice the switch - which means you would never have lit the room, which means you wouldn't have seen the door. You'd still be trying to bend those bars!

We all have different thresholds for hanging in there until..

Of course, the ideal is to have balance and to always treat ourselves with care, and when things get tough, to treat ourselves as we would a loved one who is going through a rough time.

Instead of fooooorcing ourselves to keep going, take some time out, "lie down on the bed and sleep" - which stands for doing whatever feels good at the time, whether it is sleeping, or whether it's watching T.V. or a movie (as long as it makes you feel good ;)) or whether it's a bubble bath or a walk, or playing a game, or going bungee jumping, or having some other kind of fun, or just getting into cozy clothes with a hot chocolate and reading a book - whatever feeeels good.

The fear we have is that we will become lazy, or that it's wasted time, or that it's not helping ... when in fact, the opposite is true. When we take time off to feel good, we allow our minds to process stuff, and once we've had enough rest and time out, we find that ideas and solutions and synchronicities start to appear "out of nowhere". And some of them seem really obvious once we become aware of them - but we would never have seen them while we were struggling (you'll never see the door if you won't take your focus off the bars

So, ideally whenever you feel stressed or worried or things seem to "keep going wrong", take time out. You may only need a few minutes, or an hour, you may need the day, you may need a week, or, if things have built up to a certain point you may need two weeks or more

Some of us need to get to the stage where we've exhausted ourselves physically, mentally and emotionally to the point where "laying down on the bed and sleeping" is the ONLY option we haven't tried and we're just too drained and broken to do anything else. ;)

But of course, once that's happened, we then know that in future whenever we feel the beginnings of that situation again, even though it seems illogical to take time out - that is the solution ;)

≪ ≪ ≪ ≫ ≫ ≫

Parenting - Paying it Backwards!

This may cause some resistance and emotional reaction in some people, but I wrote it in response to several cases of adults feeling manipulated by guilt from their parents. One or two of these adults no longer wanted to spend time with their parents because they always felt low when with them, but their parents were making them feel guilty that they didn't want to see them.

Here's my view:

I've found that some of the things that hold us back in our attempts to change negative beliefs, and that prevent us from ALLOWING our desires to manifest, are rooted in programming from childhood.

It seems that a large part of the world has some of the main responsibilities of Parenting **backwards!**

Some of the core teachings I'm referring to are

* You **owe** your parents **respect, love and loyaltz**

* You **owe** your parents **gratitude** for **everything they do for you**

... And many, many parents control their children with **guilt**.

Here's what I believe to be the truth:

* Children are born with a **blank slate**, and the adults who raise the child, **write on that slate** of WHO that child IS.

* It is a parent's **job** to protect, nurture, support, guide and unconditionally love their child. It is the parent's **responsibility**

to **build** that child's **Self Esteem and Self Worth**, so that the child grows into a happy, secure, well-balanced, confident adult who is well-equipped to succeed in Relationships, Career, Finances, and in looking after themselves generally - **because they've been programmed** with the **belief** that they **genuinely deserve** to be happy.

* **You can't grow a strong, healthy tree by kicking and damaging the sapling**. You cannot raise a strong, healthy and successful adult by treating the child with **disrespect** and **sabotaging** his **self esteem** and **self worth**.

* If a child is raised with Love, Compassion, Respect, Guidance and Understanding - and **if the parent sets the example** of how they would like the child to behave and speak (children learn how to be who they are, primarily by **automatically copying** the significant adults in their lives) - the child will <u>Automatically</u> show love, respect, loyalty and love to their parents. It will come **naturally** and because the child **wants to**, not out of guilt or fear.

* It's a **natural instinct** for a child to show love, respect, and loyalty to his parent. **He's born with it.** If he doesn't show these qualities, there is something wrong with what the parents are doing.

* The **only person** you are **responsible for**, apart from **yourself**, is your **own child**. Parents are responsible for their children, not the other way 'round.

The fact that most parents have no **intention** of damaging their children, and are only **misguided** and reacting to their **own upbring**ing - **does not diminish the damage**. It does not make it in any way acceptable.

When someone kills a pedestrian, the fact that they weren't taught to drive properly, does not undo the death.

What we can do about it is, once we realize the truth, we can **stop the cycle**. We can start to **reverse the flow**. We can start to **pay the respect forward**, to our children, and let go of the guilt passed to us by our own parents.

Pack Your Bags, We're Going On a Guilt Trip:

I believe that **Guilt** is the most **common** (and **toxic**) form of control parents use against their children. And the problem is that the very nature of guilt is that **the victim feels too guilty to object to it** - and to **name it** as a guilt trip. A Guilt Trip has a built-in protection against detection! ;)

I once heard a parent lay a guilt trip on her (teenage) child about shielding her with her own body when they were in danger, when the child was a toddler. This made the teenager feel guilty, and she completely **bought into the guilt**. But, as someone else pointed out ..... um..... wouldn't ANY parent do that? - wouldn't that teenager, herself have done that for her **own child?** ..... it's **basic instinct**..... most adults, parents or not, would risk their life to save a child!

It is not something the child should be made to feel guilty about. It is not beyond the call of duty for a parent to protect their child at all costs!

What this guilt trip does is imprint upon the child that she is **unworthy** of being shown such selfless love, and should feel **grateful** for it. It is not something she deserves automatically.

This parent's point was that she'd **sacrificed** so much for her child, she'd even risked her life for her, **so how could the child be so ungrateful**. In other words, **it doesn't matter what you feel or think** - I risked my life for you and sacrificed for you and **you owe me**, so you should do as I say **regardless**.

Parents are SUPPOSED to look after their children, and if that means sacrificing, well that's part of the job description. **It does not mean the child owes the parents anything.** That child will only owe their OWN children, if they have them.

Parents need to earn the child's respect, loyalty and love - **by treating the child with** respect, loyalty and love. NOT the other way around (which is the way most of us are raised) Parents can earn the child's **respect, loyalty and love** by demonstrating it - and the child will **naturally** show those qualities! No guilt trips needed!

In other words, it's not necessary for a parent to yell and be harsh in order to get their child to mind them, there are plenty of parenting tools and advice that can help parents discipline without damage

The first step towards dealing with a guilt trip is to recognize it!

* If someone is asking you to do something that makes *you* feel bad, in order to prevent *them* from feeling bad, it's a GUILT TRIP.

* If you feel hesitant to say no because you'll hurt their feelings - and they'll make sure you know it, it's a GUILT TRIP.

* If you feel bad because someone is claiming that their happiness depends on you, it's a GUILT TRIP.

Here's the Truth:

* Every person is responsible for their OWN happiness.

* Your responsibility is to yourself, and your own children.

* Every person has a CHOICE about how they react to something. You can't MAKE someone feel anything.

f you choose not to share your life with your parents **there's a REALLY good reason for that**. It is a child's **natural instinct** to want to share with their parents. If they don't, there is something wrong with the way the parents are.

If your parents choose to behave in a way that makes you feel bad, then you have **every right** to avoid putting yourself through that. You need to protect yourself. If you have children, then you also have a responsibility to protect your children. But you do NOT have a responsibility to protect or pander to your parents.

If they choose that behavior, and you then choose to not expose yourself to it, then **everyone is making their own choices.** It is then **their choice** as to how they react and feel.

If in any doubt, ask yourself: **"Would I do that to my child?"** or **"Would I say that to anyone?"**

Most parents are **oblivious** to the **damage** they do to their children. They have **good intentions** but are **misguided** and **misinformed** – mainly because of their own upbringing. But, as mentioned above, **this does not undo the damage.**

Paying it Backwards:

The setup at the moment generally involves adults with issues dating back to the way they were raised, feeling guilt and debt to their parents, and unknowingly taking their issues out on their children. Passing gratitude and respect back up the line to their parents, and dumping the issues down the line, onto their children. This is unintentional of course, and only due to the fact that they've been programmed to do this.

Imagine switching it round. **Paying it forward**. Paying the **respect**

and **unconditional love** forward to the **children**, and placing the **responsibility for issues, backwards**, where they came from.

Imagine a whole generation growing up with High Self Esteem and High Self Worth.

Imagine a generation of new adults who feel so good about themselves that **they don't need to bring others down to feel better**; who feel so good about themselves that they are **comfortable with showing love, respect and support for others**; who feel so good about themselves, that they **ALLOW themselves to succeed** in all areas of their lives. Imagine these people **running countries** and **businesses**. Imagine these people being responsible for our world.

Here's an exercise I gave to someone who wrote to me regarding the emotional and mental abuse she'd suffered from her mother. Her mother was also laying guilt trips on her now that she's older, and she didn't want her mother in her life any more because of this, but felt too guilty to say so.

This exercise is deceptively effective!

Pick a time and place you won't be disturbed. Start writing a letter to your mother. You're not going to give it to her, so REALLY let rip. Insult, swear, be as vicious as you can. Just let everything flow uncensored. Once you've finished, read it back. If you think you might like to read it again later, put it away in a safe place.

Once you feel you're finished with it, destroy it in whatever way you want to. Some people burn it ceremoniously; some just tear it up and throw it away... whatever feels good for you. After you've written the letter and re-read it, go to sleep if you can. You will probably be emotionally exhausted, and so much is processed during sleep, the healing will accelerate while you're asleep. Then, be extra good to yourself - take it easy and pamper yourself.

Here are some tips for this exercise:

* It is MUCH more Powerful than one might predict.

* If you can't think of anything to say, just start writing anything and it will flow.

* If you start, and you really can't feel anything at the time (some people with extreme emotional damage can access their feelings easily, and others have built up a protective wall, it depends on the individual), if this is the case, wait until you are in an emotional state about something else. Wait until you feel angry, frustrated, sad, scared.... and then start the letter. Your current emotional issues ALL date back to the damage you've suffered from childhood onwards, from the person who was supposed to protect and nurture you. So when you're in the middle of an emotional state about something else, redirect it to where it belongs - your mother, and start telling her in this letter exactly what she's caused.

* Once you do start, write EVERYTHING. Some people find that, as they write, their language and writing actually reverts back to that of a child or teenager.

* Some people who have extreme self esteem damage are unable to feel for the child they were. They feel no pity or compassion, just nothing. If this is the case, imagine it's not you. Imagine the adult treated another child like this - could be a child you know, or even one you don't know. You can also imagine that your mother is a stranger. What would be your reaction if you witnessed a stranger treating her child like that?

* You could also start to write the letter pretending to be a relative, friend or neighbor who has witnessed the abuse. If you do this you may well find that once you get going, you switch to your own perspective anyway.

You may find it necessary to do this a couple of times before you get all of it out.

I would then write a second letter a few days later. This one, to be given to your mother. This one, because you've got all the emotion out in the previous one, can be more polite and calm. I would say what I feel, and explain in a matter-of-fact tone, why I won't put up with any more of this behavior. I would also tell her in the letter, that if she cannot treat me with respect, that unfortunately I'll have to limit contact with her. Whatever you feel comfortable with.

Then you can get on with focusing on the good stuff! Then you can get on with focusing on what makes you feel good, and creating what you want in your life.

Note: I wrote this before I discovered the superpower I mention in the chapter "You Have a Superpower" – I still believe the exercise of writing a letter you'll never send is extremely powerful, but I would now advise that after you've done that, you do the exercise in the Superpower chapter, rather than writing the second letter. ☺

The response from this person at the time was that she was too scared to confront her mother, even in a letter. As I say, I would now recommend not sending the second letter, and instead, doing the Superpower exercise. But here is my reply to her at that time:

I completely understand the feelings of fear at the idea of confronting your mother - even in a letter.

Don't worry about that letter right now. The most important one is the one you DON'T give to her. That's the one that starts the healing process. That's the one that will help you to get your strength back.

At this stage, all you need to do is: take some time when you're alone, get yourself a cup of tea, sit down and start writing. The rest will come. Knowing that no-one is ever going to see what you're writing should free you to express yourself fully.

I also understand the tie to your mother. You've been programmed with guilt, fear and thousands of false beliefs, including that you are responsible for your mother's well being. While you consciously recognize this isn't true, the beliefs are programmed into your subconscious, and are running on automatic. It'll take a while to change them. If you imagine instructions carved into stone, and you want to write new instructions over them, if you try and write over them as they are, the new instructions would be illegible. You'd have to file down the old instructions first, before you could then carve the new ones.

Writing the letter you don't give to your mother, is the first step in purging those false beliefs.

Here are some things I want to acknowledge - and it's good to remind yourself of them too.

* Your mother was entrusted with a precious child and her job was to protect, nurture and guide that child with love. Her most important task was to build that child's self esteem and self worth so that the child could grow into a happy, secure, successful adult.

* She did the exact opposite of that.

* The emotional and mental abuse you've suffered is as damaging (if not more damaging) than the physical abuse some parents go to jail for.

* The trauma which started when you were a baby, hasn't stopped, and you're still suffering it.

* If this was a marriage, you would be an abused wife and advised to get away from your husband.

* Your mother chooses each day, to behave, speak and react in the way she does, just as we all do.

* Your mother has the choice to change - if she REALLY wants to keep her family, friends and employees!

* If she chooses not to change, then you have to accept that this is the game she's chosen to play, and let her get on with it.

* Remind yourself that each person is creating their own physical experience. And, despite appearances, it's all about choice. Remember that some people choose to see horror movies, some choose to see comedies, and some choose to see dramas... and so on. Some people choose to do extreme sports, others prefer to read and take long walks..... If you think this way, and you remind yourself that your mother is choosing to create whatever it is she's creating - no matter how much she appears to object to it - you will eventually be able to observe her without feeling the responsibility to help her.

* If someone chooses to go bungee-jumping, and you don't want to do it, you can watch them do it, without feeling the need to catch them, or to jump with them. You can watch them get scared, and say they've changed their mind and they don't want to do it anymore, they really, really don't want to jump. And you can remind them that they don't HAVE to go through with it, they can still pull out...

.... And you can hear them say "No, but I have to do it.", and give all the excuses as to why they have to do it (when in the reality is that they

ARE able to simply take off the rope and walk away from the jump) ....
and you can then realize that they are CHOOSING to do it regardless
of what they say.

And you can then ALLOW that. And you can then watch them go
through with it, grateful that you are keeping your feet firmly on the
ground and without any guilt about not jumping with them - because
they CHOOSE to do it, and YOU CHOOSE not to. If your mother has
chosen to do bungee jumping when she doesn't need to, and she claims
that since she's doing it, you have to jump with her, and you don't want
to do it, then there is absolutely NO reason you should! She has the
choice to do or not do. And so do you.

* No matter what your mother says, she has LITERALLY chosen
(and continues to choose) to: divorce, loose her son, loose her business,
be hated by her employees, be filled with debt, loose her family, and she
is ABSOLUTELY choosing to loose her daughter. She is CHOOSING
to "suffer" by choosing to stick to the behavior and attitude that have
got her this far.

* Now, you CHOOSE what you do next. You choose to heal yourself,
and you choose to build your self esteem. And once you've written that
letter that you don't give her, you will find that you begin to feel the
healing start.

* And once you've started healing yourself, you'll find the strength
to limit your contact with your mother (with or without that second
letter ;)), and you'll find your other relationships, work issues... and
EVERYTHING else will improve automatically - because ALL of it is
tied into your self esteem.

* The way your mother has treated you, and continues to treat you, is

ABSOLUTELY WRONG! There is NO excuse for it, and there is NO reasoning for it. It is WRONG.

* You deserve SO much better. You deserve the best. You deserve people who love and cherish you, who appreciate you, and who respect you. The fact that she is your mother does NOT entitle her to your shiny presence! If she really wants you in her life, she can choose to change her behavior.

≪ ≪ ≪ ≫ ≫ ≫

You Have a Superpower!

Did you know you have a Superpower? Just like comic book heroes. Each of us has it, but most don't know they have it, never mind how to use it.

The method of using this power is very, very simple, but it does take a change in perspective - and it does take practice.

Firstly, your superpower has been disguised and misunderstood. When you are channeling your power the feeling you feel is what we call "unconditional love". Now that may sound wafty, but just bear with me for a moment.

Here's an analogy:

When it's cold, and you switch the heating on, you then feel warmth. The feeling of warmth is just a feeling - it's a result not a cause. The heating is the cause. You switched the heating on and that made you feel warm. Unconditional love is the result, it's not the cause. You feel it when you're channeling your power.

When you stand under the shower, you get wet. The shower is the cause and you only get wet when you stand under it. When you step out of the shower you will eventually dry off.

So it is with your superpower. When you are channeling your power, you feel unconditional love. When you're not, you don't feel it. Because we can't see our power, it's like not being able to see the water. We move around until we feel wet. ;)

With practice it becomes very easy to instantly channel your Superpower by bringing up that feeling of "unconditional love". Then you can aim it at specific situations, people and issues - and it honestly is like magic! For example, if you're worried about a phone call you have to make, you can conjure up your superpower (and of course, you'll feel it as unconditional love), and you can aim it at the phone call you're about to make, as well as the person you'll be speaking to. The result will ALWAYS be either good, or at the very least nothing to worry about.

How to Use Your Superpower

Here are a few ways to conjure your Superpower... and I'm sure you'll find more...

Because we can't see our Superpower, the best way to conjure it up is by practicing conjuring up Unconditional Love - and when we get it right, we'll be able to tell by how it feels, and will then be able to aim it and use it effectively.

Unconditional Love is of course love without condition. This can be trickier than one might expect at first. But with practice it becomes REALLY easy - because once you have the hang of it, it's **no longer a mental thing - or even an emotional thing** - <u>it is literally a</u> <u>Superpower you use rather than an emotion you feel.</u>

But to begin with, in order to reach the point where you can use it in this way, you need to learn to conjure it up using Unconditional Love as an emotion first. So here are some ideas...

You can practice firstly by thinking of someone or something (or even an activity) that you really love - that you love just because they/it exist/s. Then slowly change that person/ thing in your mind - imagine that the specific things you like are no longer there or are different - and still love that person/thing/activity. Do this one thing at a time, slowly, and make sure you feel that expansive feeling (that's the feeling of your power physically flowing through you!) before moving on to the next change.

Here's an example:

I love my son. Not because of any of his characteristics (although I love those about him as well), but just because he's him. Just because he exists. Now, my son is very positive and enthusiastic, so I start by imagining that he is a bit more laid-back and not responsive. I imagine giving him a gift, and instead of the usual gratitude and excitement, I imagine he just takes it in a non-interested way and without even saying thank you. Now I hold that image of him and consciously feel love and compassion for that version of him, just as it is. Then I imagine him being really difficult and miserable… and I consciously focus on loving that version of him as well. And so I work on focusing on feeling love for that version of my son regardless of whether he's appreciative or not.

Another example:

Perhaps you love a particular holiday spot and would love to go there. Let's say the Bahamas. You've dreamed of going there for a holiday. Now imagine you've been told you'll never go to the Bahamas. Now love the Bahamas anyway. Love it just because it exists, even though you know you'll never go there. Love that it exists for others, and just for itself.

At first this may seem impossible with certain things or people, but it IS possible (I do it every day with things that seem impossible to love unconditionally and it's now easy!) **It just takes practice**. That's all. Think of it like learning to ride a bicycle - and each time you don't manage to feel the feeling, or you lose it, remind yourself that you just fell of the bike and you're still learning, and then get back on! ☺

Sometimes you'll start to feel it and then lose it again - get back on the bike and find it again… and with practice you'll be able to hold it for longer and longer until it's literally "on tap" like mine is. ☺ Eventually you won't have to work at it, you won't have to tryyyy, you'll be able to literally point, aim and do it - just like a Superpower! ☺

Here's a daily exercise you can do to develop your skill in using your superpower:

1. Pick a time (morning works best because it sets you up perfectly for the rest of the day), when you can sit quietly and undisturbed.

2. Start with your body. Your body is made up of around 50 trillion individual cells. Each one working as an individual within the whole. Doing its own job in order to serve the whole.

Each one has a consciousness. Start by sending Unconditional Love to each of those cells.

All you need in order to do this, is to think of those cells with compassion. Love them just for existing. **They don't even have to do anything to deserve your love, you just love them because they are.**

This is a little bit like tuning in a radio station - it can take a little while to hit the right vibration.... and when you do, you will feel it **physically**, in your chest. You'll feel an expanding feeling. Just like you do when you think of someone you love unconditionally.

3. Once you feel this, the aim is to try and keep it going for as long as you can. As I said before, it'll be like learning to ride a bicycle - you'll be on and off, but just keep getting back on, and the more you practice, the longer you'll be able to hold it at a time.

4. Then move on to people in your life - send this Unconditional Love to a person. Remember, the Power is in the Unconditional love - love just for existing, regardless of any outcome or result. Sometimes I sense this Power as a gold light - it may be different for everyone... the important thing is that it's the feeling of Unconditional Love.

5. Next, move on to things you're worried about.... to each of these situations, send that Unconditional Love. Love for the situation - **regardless of how it will turn out** - that's the tricky bit - regardless of how it will turn out! ;)

The Unconditional Bit:

This is the key, and it's what makes all the difference - love for the situation you're worried about, **regardless of how it will turn out**.... what you're effectively doing there, is channeling your Power (the feeling of unconditional love is the feeling of your Power coursing through you!), and aiming it at the situation - and opening up to, and allowing the best possible outcome, regardless of what it is.

Then, no matter what the outcome turns out to be (and it will most of the time be the one you were wanting anyway - as long as you detach from it), it will be perfect for you - often in ways you'd never have dreamed of! ;)

You can aim it at your bank account and/or your wallet and/or money in general. Remember to keep it UNCONDITIONAL - so, not a lot of money, not a healthy bank account, but just money in general, just the very existence of it, even if it never comes your way, just love it for existing; your bank account just for existing - exactly as it is. Just as you would love a baby just because it is. Your child just because he exists. **Unconditional** Love.

Again, it takes practice. It's quite a challenge, when we're worried about something, or when we don't want something, to send unconditional love to it. It's difficult to not latch onto an outcome.... but in the moment you latch onto a specific outcome, you're closing off the Power. If you send conditional love, instead of unconditional love (in other words you are attached to a particular outcome (condition)) then in that moment, you've tuned out... you need to tune back into the unconditional love - that is the Power. It's tricky to begin with, **but with practice, it becomes easier and easier!**

Using the shower analogy I used above: Because the shower is invisible, you need to keep moving around until you feel wet, and then, if you don't feel wet anymore you know you've stepped out of the shower again, so move around again until you feel wet again... and eventually you'll learn exactly where the shower is, and you'll be able to walk into that room anytime, and straight under the shower whenever you want to. ☺

If you do this each day, preferably in the morning (and you can aim that Power at your whole day ahead of you, and anything specific you're concerned about coming up that day) you will find you become more and more Powerful, and you get better and better at it. And then, as you go about your day, when something comes up that you're not happy about, or that bothers you or worries you, conjure up that Power - that feeling of unconditional love that you've been practicing, and aim it at whatever the issue is... you'll be amazed at the effect and speed of the results!

I have now got to the stage (with lots of practice and falling off the bicycle and getting back on lol ;)), where, when something happens during my day that worries me, or that I don't want.... I catch myself in the moment of reaction - and I correct it.

Sometimes I'll start off with a negative reaction, but then I remind myself, and I'm now able to stop, conjure up my Superpower, and aim it, just like a fire-hose, at that situation or person - and it is unbelievable some of the results I've seen - things I'd never have imagined!

Things turn around, change, time stands still, people change, unexpected things happen.... it all works out perfectly, **despite the original impression!**

Remember that it takes practice, so it's important to **be gentle with yourself** - just as you would if you were teaching a child to ride a bicycle. Keep practicing, keep getting back in line, in tune, in balance in this way.

Dealing With the "Don't Wants"

I've written a lot about our Power and how we can channel it - kinda like a super-hero - and how we can change things with it. The name we've given to the feeling we get when we're channeling our Power is "Unconditional Love".

Someone said to me the other day that he understands from what he's learned about the Law of Attraction, that you should not think about what you don't want, only about what you do want.

Now, that's a good idea, except that by denying (and resisting) the "don't want" you're of course attracting it. Even by stopping yourself from thinking of it.

Here's what I believe gives us REAL Power:

Think about your "don't want"... and then aim Unconditional Love at it - regardless of how it turns out. Do this on purpose. If you're worried about a phone call you have to make, think about that phone call, and consider how badly it could go... and then Love that outcome - Unconditionally! It's like MAGIC!! I've been doing this on and off for a while now, but recently I've managed to do it more consistently and it honestly is Magic! Either the thing turns out the way I wanted it too anyway, or something completely different happens - but always good in the end! ☺

Now, I've said all this before, but HERE's my latest discovery:

Love the way you reacted to the situation - even when you

reacted negatively! Now THIS is Gold! I was getting frustrated with myself for getting frustrated with specific situations, when I know my power lies in sending unconditional love to them, but I just couldn't help myself sometimes - I just felt soooo angry (it doesn't happen often anymore - I'm happier than I've ever been, but there are still certain things that push my buttons).... And then, the other day it occurred to me - the **Ultimate** is to **Love the negative** as well as the positive - **Unconditionally!**

And so I now send Unconditional Love <u>to the way I reacted</u> as well as to the situation itself. And the results are like being in a fairy tale! ☺

Fear of aiming Unconditional Love at "don't wants" - isn't that encouraging more of them?

Someone asked me this question last night - if you feel good about the "bad stuff", isn't that attracting more of the bad stuff? It's a good question, and a natural feeling - I've had it myself, I saw it a bit like: Someone comes up and slaps you, and you say "Wow, thanks, I really appreciate that"... and so they slap you again! ;)

However, your Superpower doesn't work like that - our brains work like that, but not the Superpower.

A good analogy for the answer to this question is:

When you learn to swim, if you fight the water you are more likely to go under. In order to overcome it, you have to relax, accept it and then you can learn to float.

And when you find yourself in rough seas, the more you fight it the more chance you have of drowning, but if you are able to relax and float, and then swim, you'll be more likely to last it out until it calms down, or you find your way to shore or a rescue boat. Hey, with practice, you'll eventually be able to not only float and swim, you'll be surfing those waves.

Now, by learning to float, you're not going to create MORE rough water, you'll just be able to cope better with the rough water that's already there anyway. And in fact, floating will create calm whereas flailing about and fighting it will create more turmoil.

So, when the "bad stuff" comes along, fighting it will create more turmoil, and you'll find it much more difficult to last through the storm and find your way to shore, whereas if you practice feeling unconditional love towards the "bad stuff" - that's like learning to float. And then to swim. It'll make the bad stuff less dramatic, and in fact, the bad stuff will usually turn out to be good stuff! ;)

So when you feel worried that feeling good about something "bad" that's happening, is going to encourage more of that to happen, change your perspective to think "I'm not encouraging more of it, I'm floating. This feeling of Unconditional Love is the feeling of floating on the rough water until it calms or I reach land/ a rescue boat ... or I find a way to surf it!"

An important point to remember:

You cannot send love to anyone or anything else unless you're already full of it yourself ;)

If you don't have plenty of it yourself, you have very little - if any - to give. So you need to **first fill yourself with unconditional love - for YOURSELF** - THEN let it flow over and expand to other people and situations etc.

So here's what I started doing: I imagine turning on a faucet which activates a shower of gold light (the power which feels like unconditional love). That shower of gold light pours into me, filling me right up with the gold light - which feels like unconditional love - for myself. Then, once I feel filled with unconditional love for myself - and ONLY then - I start imagining it spreading outwards, filling the room I'm in and then on to fill people, situations, the room I'm going to be in later today etc. It took me a day of focusing ONLY on filling myself with this love - without attempting to send it anywhere else - before I was filled up enough to then start sending it.

The challenges I mentioned (which involve other people's actions) have literally turned around completely. It's really incredible! And whenever there's any kind of doubt, I turn on that shower. And whenever I think of it during the day, I turn on the shower.

So, the key is to fill yourself with unconditional love FIRST. It may take a few hours, a few days or even weeks of filling only yourself with that power, before you are topped up enough to then send it out to others and to situations. I'm certain it will depend on the individual.

"My cup runneth over" has just popped into my mind. ;)

Handy Tip for Using Your Superpower:

If, each time you practice switching on your Power, you say a particular phrase (you could use anything from something as simple as "I love you" to the Ho'oponopono phrase "I'm sorry, please forgive me, I forgive you, thank you, I love you".... to the SGI Buddhist chant "Nam myoho renge kyo".... to something completely arbitrary like " Sausages" ;) - if you repeat the same word or phrase each time you practice switching on your Power, your brain will form an automatic (and physical) connection between that word/phrase, and the Power flow.

This means that when you say that word or phrase, your brain will automatically create the physiological process that accompanies your surge of Power (the feeling unconditional love). ....

And the reason this is so great is: **It means that when you're feeling anything but loving** - when you're feeling angry, hurt, frustrated, tired, upset etc. and you can't muster up the strength to channel your Power, you can simply say the phrase or word, and THAT will **trigger your brain to create the response automatically!** ☺

Just like certain smells, music and even colors can create an emotional response in us, we can train our brains to respond to a certain word or phrase with the feeling of unconditional love. ☺

Another Handy Tip for Using Your Superpower:

When things are getting stressful, try changing your perception slightly, to see life as a giant computer game - and your superpower (unconditional love) is like the shooty thing (you can tell I'm an expert at computer games ;)) ... and see all the obstacles that arise as targets for shooting your superpower of unconditional love at. ☺

Here's a little exercise that's quite fun to do:

When you're in a public place - waiting in a line in a store, or at a bus stop - start filling yourself with your superpower (remember, you need to start with unconditional love for yourself - starting with all your cells is quite effective). You could visualize a gold shower of light, or whatever works for you. Then, when you're completely full up with it, allow it to radiate out from you, filling the room or area you're in, including filling up all the people.... and see what happens. ;)

Remember to keep it <u>unconditional</u> - love regardless of results.

Superpower Q & A

When I first spoke of, and wrote about, this topic, I received a lot of questions – some of which I thought useful to include in this book ...

Q: I am quite a positive person but, every now and again I find myself doing things or saying things that are at odds with what I believe.

A: Yes, I have to say, even though I've been using this for quite a while now, and have become quite good at it almost all of the time ... there are one or two instances where I still find it quite a challenge! Think of when you learned to ride a bicycle and you were finally riding around without falling off,... and then you find you have to ride up a steep hill ;)

As long as you keep getting back on, it doesn't matter how many times you fall off.☺

Q: Will this work on situations of attracting a specific person? For example if I want a certain someone to like me back, and I send love to him will it work?

A: Only if the love is unconditional ;) ... which is the tricky bit if you want him to like you of course. You have to get to a place where you love him whether he likes you or not. Start with the exercise "How to Use Your Superpower", and then aim that power at him, then - and this is the vital bit - imagine he doesn't like you, imagine he'll never like you, and love him anyway! If you make sure the love is **unconditional** you'll get the result you want. It will take practice, but it gets easier.☺

Q: Do you think I can use this to get my ex back? And so that he wants to be faithful to me?

A: Well, you can certainly use this to create for yourself, a happy, healthy, fulfilling and loving relationship - whether that's with your ex or with someone new.

Use the method of conjuring up your Superpower - start by, first of all (and this is VITAL) filling **Yourself** with unconditional love. And once you've done that, then do the sending of unconditional love to your ex (remember it must be **Unconditional** ;)) And then you will either experience the relationship you want from him, or you will lose the need to be with him and find that relationship with someone who does give you exactly what you want (because it will be YOU giving yourself what you want ;))

Q: What does it mean when you don't attract anyone into your life, good or bad. I'm married and have a child but have no friends, I rarely see my family and I desperately feel that I need friends.

A: It starts where everything else starts - begin to practice channeling unconditional love for yourself. Once you are practicing this, you will automatically find people drawn to you, as well as opportunities for meeting people who "click" with you, and you will automatically create strong, rewarding friendships. ☺

Q: I have now started sending unconditional love to my mother-in-law, who I've hated for so long. I am sending her love and visualizing her being so nice to me, being kind to me and loving me. Is it truly possible to change people/circumstances no matter how complicated if we bless and love them?

A: WELL DONE YOU! ☺ I'm so excited and happy for you - it sounds like you've really had a major breakthrough!

One tip - it's important to make sure the love you are sending is

Unconditional - which means being very well aware that even if they don't love you back, even if your mother-in-law doesn't change, you love her just for existing, because she is a part of you. She is a magnificent spiritual being playing the role of your mother-in-law in your story, and if she's playing the "baddie" character this time round, then you can appreciate how well she's playing it. It's VERY important to make sure that the love is **Unconditional** - that you love her regardless **of whether she changes or stays exactly as she is**........ And the most INCREDIBLE thing is: **THAT is when she'll change. ;)**

In my (extensive) experience with this, I have found that the times when people have changed or situations have changed, it has ALWAYS been when I have ensured that the love I'm sending is **Unconditional** - that I am feeling love **regardless of the outcome**. Then the outcome is always in my favor. ☺ It's a funny paradox, but it seems to be the way it works. ☺

Q: This has got me thinking... if you can change the way a person behaved towards you... then can you choose exactly how they behave towards you??? for example, could you regularly send love to a person and imagine them sucking up to you all the time and then it would happen?? haha i know people might have opinions about that, but come on everyone has that one person they would love to suck up to them for once hahaha what do u think??? can u actually create certain specific behaviors with people and make relationships exactly as you want them?? you must be able to :P

A: A good question ☺

Considering we can each only create within our own life experience, I believe this is how it would work:

Sally wants Jim to go out of his way for her - to spoil her and treat her like a queen.

Sally wanting this is not necessarily going to "make" it happen.

Sally starts sending unconditional love to Jim - meaning she loves him **just for existing, not on condition he treats her the way she wants to be treated.** In fact, as part of her unconditional love-sending process, she actually imagines him **not doing what she wants,** and **makes sure she loves that outcome too**!

Once Sally has got the hang of this, one of two things happen:

If it is part of the life experience Jim subconsciously wants to have, or if it is part of the subconscious programming from when he was a child, Jim will start to *want* to treat Sally the way she wants to be treated.

If it is not part of Jim's life experience, Sally will find that someone else starts to treat her in the way she wanted Jim to treat her - she'll lose the attachment to Jim automatically, and will feel the same (or more strongly) about the new person. ☺

Q: Illusions, while reading your article, I remember that a few months ago I came to the same conclusion regarding my physical body. I mean, when I look in the mirror I see some things that I do not like, like a lot of extra weight, really uneven skin tone on my face, massive hair breakage, etc, etc and I came to the conclusion that this was a reflection/ projection of what I think deep down (perhaps not that deep lol), wether I liked it or not and wether I knew it or not. I had intended to work on that but then I had other things to work on that needed my immediate attention to this day.

So I was wondering if you had any articles or thoughts about that. Thank you.

A: I agree - everything we experience outside ourselves is a reflection of what's inside. The way to change the outside is by changing the inside of course. So, practice looking at yourself in the mirror, and loving every bit of you - **just as it is**.

If you find it difficult at first, here's a way that can make it easier to start with: See past the physical level you're able to see (if that makes sense J) - your body is made up of billions of cells, all working together - each one doing its bit for the whole, each one working to the best of its ability for the benefit of the whole. Start by focusing on those selfless, little hard-workers - start by appreciating and loving them. Each one. Once you've got the unconditional love flowing for them, it's easier to spread it out over the levels to finally appreciate and love the whole just as it is.

Hope that makes sense?

By aiming unconditional love at the outside - meaning loving it just as it is, not wishing for it to be different - you are changing your whole vibration, your state, and of course over time, the results of this change inside will start to show on the outside. But it can take time, so keep going. With practice it becomes your dominant state. At first you'll have to consciously remind yourself to do it, like an exercise, but the more you do it, the more natural it will become and eventually it will become the state you're in most of the time, barring the ups and downs of normal life experience ☺

Also, once you've done the bit in front of a mirror, you don't have to be in front of a mirror to do it - you can aim the power at your body at any time. Sitting in an office, waiting for a bus, shopping in the grocery store.... Do it as often as you can and whenever you think of it.

《 《 《 》 》 》

If You Can't be with the Things You Love, Love the Things You Hate

When you first discover that you're actually in full control of your life, and that you can make changes to aspects of your life you thought were out of your control, it can be frustrating when you're making the changes but not seeing the results yet. Many people have a (perfectly human) tendency to lose confidence in themselves and their ability to get the results they want. The tricky thing is that there is a time delay (as explained in previous chapters), and during that time delay, if you stop what you're doing and go back to the "old way" of thinking and behaving, you'll lose the momentum you built up. Like the digging up of the seed. So the challenge is to keep going until you see results.

Here's a perspective you can adopt that can help you to keep going until you start seeing the results you want:

When stuff pops up that you don't want – whether it's situations, other people's actions, "failures" or old patterns – remind yourself to take every worry, concern, fear, frustration, fury, disappointment... and any other "don't want"... as an opportunity to "clear" it by channeling unconditional love at it. So, exactly the process detailed in the chapter "You Have a Superpower" and in the 7 Day Experiment towards the end of this book(starting with all the cells etc.), but doing it throughout the day, in the moment, at any "don't want" - **just like shooting moving targets at a fair**. ;)

Seeing each "don't want" that comes up as a moving target at a fair stall - and shooting it with unconditional love - turning the horrible feeling into a feeling of relief and even fun! ☺

Q: Maybe what you mean is to except everything for just the way they are. If it is, it sure take lots of work but when i finally hit it, I will feel in peace. But sometimes i tend to forget doing this too lol

A: Yes, it is a form of accepting - but it's more than that, it's Loving it! ;) It is tricky to begin with, which is why I wrote the process in the 7 day experiment - that helps to get into the right feeling, and practicing it every day for even just 7 days can make it much easier to access that feeling. With practice it becomes less about emotion and more about power.

Some might say it becomes a method of getting around the ego's perception of "unconditional love" and recognizing it as a power, not an emotion. ;) The ego sees "love" and "unconditional love" as an emotion, because the result of channeling the power is a "feeling". But the feeling is only the result of the power - like feeling warmer is only the result of turning up the heating, the heater is not the feeling, it is the power that causes the feeling.

It doesn't take as much work as you might think. Check out the exercise in the 7 day experiment and do it each day for 7 days, and see how much easier it becomes. Eventually it becomes literally like flicking a switch to conjure up that feeling in any situation.

≪ ≪ ≪ ≫ ≫ ≫

How Others Treat You is Their Karma, How You React is Yours ☺

I came across this phrase and thought it was worth including. It's a great reminder to "keep your eyes on your own work" as my sister once said. What others are doing (whether it's affecting you or not) is causing their results. The way you react and respond is causing your own. It's a good phrase to print out and put up on the fridge! ☺

Q: So does this mean, say if a person got angry with you? Then you take the calm approach and not respond or retaliate? Send love to that person or white light?

A: Absolutely! And to go one better, make the white light unconditional love - in other words, be aware of loving that person regardless of what they do, say or think. Become aware of the fact that you love them just for existing. ☺

In the beginning this is a challenge and requires effort and concentration... but eventually it can become an automatic response - you can train your brain to respond automatically in this way!

And one more thing on this – at times when you don't manage to do this (and if you're human, there will be those times lol) be accepting of that – send unconditional love to yourself regardless of how you reacted. In other words, send unconditional love to the part of you that reacted negatively – that's the point (and the power) of unconditional love. And it's most powerful when you send it to yourself! ☺

Q: I am wondering am I to not react when I find my boyfriend enjoys talking with his ex girlfriend on the phone. Its not that I am jealous of her. I am baffled as to why I have to hear excitement and enthusiasm when he talks to her and doesnt have the same intent with me?

A: Keeping in mind everything outside ourselves is governed by what's happening inside us, and considering what you resist persists, the more energy you give to the way you currently feel about this situation, the more you are feeding it, and the stronger it will grow.

Here's the solution – and although it's very simple, it isn't necessarily easy, BUT it will work if you do it correctly: When you have some time on your own, sit with your eyes closed for a few minutes, and do the exercise in the chapter "You Have a Superpower" – make sure you start with yourself, and fill yourself up completely first. Next, see your power extending out from you to fill the room you're in, then fill the day ahead. Finally, see, in your mind, your boyfriend talking to his ex on the phone, as you have done, and now extend that power of unconditional love (visualize it as a light if it helps – use whatever is effective in bringing up that feeling in you) – see that power filling your boyfriend from his feet, all the way up to his head – focus on loving your boyfriend completely unconditionally (remember, this is a power, not an emotion, and not logic).

It will slip (a lot) of course, but keep bringing yourself back to that feeling – just as if you were learning to ride a bicycle and keep falling off - or tuning into a radio station and keep going past the spot. Get back on the bike. Move the tuning dial back and forth until it stays on that wave-length.

Do this exercise each morning. And when you feel the same old feelings coming up, allow them, then remind yourself of your power, and try to conjure it up right then, in the moment if you can. If you can't, don't worry, do it later. Basically, the more you do this, the easier it gets, and the faster you see results. But, remember, the love has to be unconditional – in other words, you are sending love regardless of whether anything changes or not. It is a paradox, but it's how it works. J Once you've mastered this, extend your power to your boyfriend's ex. Send the unconditional love to her as well. If you do this, and practice it (have patience with yourself), and you make sure you start with unconditional love for yourself first (that may take a little while in itself), you will see miracles! ☺

≪ ≪ ≪ ≫ ≫ ≫

How to Change Other People's Attitude, Behavior and Actions....

There IS a way to change other people - completely. But there's a specific (simple) skill to it, which can be tricky to master, but once you do, it becomes easier and easier. I'll answer the "free will" issue at the end. ;)

There are a couple of points to bear in mind when dealing with other people:

1. **<u>Everyone and everything is connected</u> - the people you want to change are connected to you on a quantum level - this means you can influence them on that level regardless of what is said or done on the "physical" level.**

There's a lot of information on the connection of all things on a quantum level. One of the most accessible and tangible explanations of this is Masaru Emoto's experiments with water crystals. *(You can find a link to Emoto's website in the Resources section of this book, if you'd like to read more about this)* If intention can affect water in that way - and considering, apart from anything else, we consist mainly of water - imagine what it can do to us! The other great resource for more information on the science between the connection of everything is Bruce Lipton's "Biology of Belief"

Sending intentions (feelings) of unconditional love, gratitude and appreciation to others can affect them on a core level - regardless of what is said or done.

2. <u>**Your environment, (including the people you come into contact with) is a reflection of what is inside you**</u> - that can often be a REALLY difficult pill to swallow lol. When someone is doing something that is hurting you, it can be practically impossible to accept (or even entertain the idea) that you are in fact doing it to yourself.

When someone does or says something that makes you angry, upset, frustrated, sad or hurt, it can be difficult to accept that if you consider that everything "outside" of you in your experience is a **reflection** of what is inside of you, there must be something inside of you that is resulting in the experience you're having with that person.. This can be empowering (if you're able to accept it) because it means that no matter how absurd it seems (why would I do that to myself?) you can control and change it. By changing your own inside, the outside will change automatically.

3. <u>**Only you can create in your own experience**</u>, no-one else.

Regardless of what anyone else does or says, only you can create in your own experience. And the way you control that is in your choice of thoughts and feelings. If someone steals my car, the natural and human reaction is for me to be angry, upset, indignant...... and those feelings will give the impression that the thief, by his actions, has caused me to be in that state. However, knowing what I know, if I choose to feel happy (I know it seems weird, but with practice it's possible to conjure up happiness and unconditional love at the drop of a hat as a physiological response instead of an emotion), I have just taken control of my experience and am choosing to feel good. The thief has no control over how I feel - he only has control over his own feelings and actions. And the Power of my happiness will have a knock-on effect on how the rest of my day goes, and how things progress from there.

So, now to the actual method of changing others:

Considering all of the above points, changing others is as simple (and as difficult) as choosing to see only what you <u>want</u> to see. Choosing to feel only what you want to feel. Sending unconditional love to the person and the situation regardless of what they do or say (think Jesus ☺) This is of course a challenge, to say the least, but when you do manage to do it, you will witness the most amazing miracles! People WILL change.

The trick is to stick it out during the time lapse. It often takes time for the effects to reach the "physical" level, so it's important to keep doing what you're doing even if you don't see a change yet (remember the seed growing beneath the surface).

What about free will?

Because each of us can only create in our own experience, we cannot single-handedly change the experience of another (we can contribute, but it is that person who is in control, whether they're aware of it or not). Therefore, it is **my** experience of that person I am changing, not their own experience. (if that makes sense?)

Here's an example:

Janet is upset because her work colleague, Sue, is impatient and irritable with her. Here are two choices for Janet:

1. She recognizes Sue's impatience and irritability and feels upset and hurt by it. She goes through, in her mind, how unfair it is, she thinks about all the reasons she doesn't deserve this, she replays all of the scenarios in which Sue has behaved in this way and retraces every

word Sue has said.....

or

2. Janet takes a mental step back. She recognizes that what is outside of her is a reflection of what is inside, and that no-one else can create in her experience; she takes a deep breath, and then starts by sending unconditional love to herself - to every cell in her body. Once she feels full of unconditional love herself, she starts to send it to Sue. It makes no difference for a while, on the physical level, but Janet knows that on a quantum level things are starting to take effect.

Now, the free will bit....

Sue's experience won't necessarily change (unless she's open to it), but Janet's experience of her will. Janet will find that either Sue is no longer impatient or irritable with her, or Sue moves on in some way and is no longer in Janet's experience. Either way, Janet will be creating a positive experience for herself.

Unconditional Love and Bullying – a Teenager's Experience

I received a message from a teenage girl who wrote to me a while go, asking me to help her to use unconditional love (which I was writing about at the time) to change issues with bullying etc. at school.

Her experience is so inspiring, I asked her if I could share it to help others realize the possibilities. Here is our correspondence through messages on a forum:

Sent Sep 21, 2011

Hi, i read ur discussion on "How to Change Other People's Attitude, Behavior and Actions", i loved it it was so helpful thx so much for posting it!!! i just got one question its the freewill part

u said that if u send unconditional love and the other person is open to change then they will change and if their not open then they'll move on and won't be in ur experience, what does it mean by wont be in ur experience? so when they move on does that mean that their not in ur life? like they moved away or something?

so if theres a girl at school thats doesnt respect me and i want her to respect me what i do is send unconditional love to her and myself and if shes open to it she'll respect me and if shes not open to it she'll be out of my experience ? like out of my life so she'll move away or something? im just confused with the move on part lol

anyway thx for posting that its really helpful!!!

My Reply:

September 22nd 2011

Hi ☺

I'm so glad you found the post useful. I should really have clarified: What I mean is that the person won't necessarily not be in your life at all, but you won't experience the same stuff with them. So, for example:

This girl who is disrespectful to you.

You send unconditional love, first to yourself and then to her (make sure it is unconditional - in other words, you're not attached to a particular outcome, so even if she were to continue being disrespectful, you would still be sending her unconditional love ;)).

If she's open to change, she will change in herself. If she's not open to change, she will either not be around you at all (she may move away, or just, synchronicity may mean that you happen to not be in the same place at the same time), or she won't be around you when she's in that frame of mind/mood.

In other words, because YOU are creating and attracting in your own experience, you will happen to be elsewhere when she's displaying the behavior that doesn't fit in with the experiences you're creating for yourself. You won't need to make an effort to physically avoid her or anything, it will just be synchronicity and the way things work out - go with the flow and keep following what feels good.

Does that make sense? Let me know if not. ☺

Love and Light and Magic xxx

September 28th 2011

Subject: How do I send unconditional love to large group of unknown people

so i've look into unconditional love and i understand how to send *unconditional love to one specific person but how do i send it to a large group of unknown people? when i'm sending it to a specific person i know my target and it makes it easier but when i'm sending it to a large group of people then its very general and its hard to focus i'm a bit confused cause i want to send unconditional love to the kids at school so they'll stop making fun of me over the rumor so how do i do that? do i think of all the kids at school in general and love all of them for just existing? im kinda lost lol*

<u>My Reply</u>:

September 29th 2011

Good Morning ☺

Here's the way I do it:

* Before you go to school in the morning, either when you first wake up, or when you're in the bath or shower, take a few moments to close your eyes and relax.

* Start with yourself. Imagine a gold light coming down from above you, like a shower, like you're standing or sitting or lying in a shower that consists of gold light energy instead of water.

* Imagine that gold light energy is unconditional love. Imagine it filling you up with unconditional love, feel love for all the cells in your body, just for existing. Each cell is working hard, doing its best for the "whole" (you) ☺

* Now imagine that gold light energy that has the feeling of unconditional love starting to radiate out from you and fill the room you're in. Feel the feeling of expansion.

* Now imagine seeing yourself in school that day. Doesn't matter where, and you don't have to actually see yourself (depends if you're a visual person - I'm more of a feeling person), you can just get a "sense" of seeing yourself at

school if you like.

* *Watch that gold energy light shower coming down into "that" you, filling her up, and expanding out, filling the hall or room, and filling every person in that hall or room - you don't have to know who they are, just know there are people there and whoever they are, they are being filled with this gold light energy that feels like unconditional love.*

* *Now imagine that that gold energy light is filling those people no matter what they're like. Be aware in your head that even if those people are mean to you today, that gold light energy of unconditional love will still fill them anyway. (That's the unconditional bit lol - and it's very important).*

I do this before any meeting or occasions I'm worried about. I see myself in the venue (even if I've never been to the venue - it doesn't matter because it's just a sense of being there, doesn't have to have detail), and I see "that" me being filled with the light, and filling the whole venue including everyone in it. And then I think to myself even if they hate me, I love them anyway and they are filled with that gold light energy anyway.

There have been a few times when it's been a bit blah - where they haven't been very enthusiastic, and when that happens, I see the gold energy light right then in the moment, imagine it filling me up, and then the whole venue including everyone in it.... and every time I've done that, the people have changed and it's turned out to be great! ☺

This looks like a long exercise, but it can actually be very quick - and it gets quicker the more you do it.

Hope it helps, let me know how it goes. X

September 29th 2011

cool im going to try this right now!! ill do this everyday before school!!! thx for ur help u explained it really well!! =)

The next message I received from her was this one, January 15th 2012:

"Subject: Unconditional love changed my life!!!

Hey we haven't talked for so long, i haven't been on here for awhile iv been busy with school i forgot my password but just recently i found my password in my super messy room so im back on!!!

Anyway i just wanted to say thank you thank you thank you for teaching me unconditional love!!! My life changed like crazy iv used unconditional love on so many experiences and it worked 100%, it took a bit time at first but then i got it and it worked, i changed the way everyone at school treats me(like everyone) and i got really succesful at everything im in every school activity the teachers love me the students love me my parantes love me im getting straight A's and best of all im not being bullied i changed everyone that didnt like me before its like im in another world and i love it! "

How fabulously inspiring is that. ☺

« « « » » »

Exercises and Experiments

I've detailed a few exercises and experiments throughout this book, and here are a few more you might like to try:

The 7 Day Experiment

It's only 7 days, and if you completely commit to it, I'm certain that at the end of the 7 days, you'll have seen such Magic that you'll want to continue

It costs nothing but a few minutes a day, a willingness to practice, and a desire and determination to stick to it no matter what - for at least just 7 days.

Here's the program:

Daily Morning Exercise - to be done as close to first thing in the morning as possible - I usually have a cup of tea first, and then do this

* Go to http://www.paths-lifeboost.com scroll down and click on "Click here and try it FREE!" - "Mood Elevation - Increase Happiness and Joy"

* If you have stereo headphones, use them for this. If not, just turn the sound down.

* Press F11 on your computer keyboard to make the screen full-size.

* Select whichever color you like - it doesn't matter which one you choose, just choose the one you like.

*Adjust the "Kinesthetic Input" slider to whatever feels most comfortable to you.

* Relax your body, and while you're watching and listening, start to channel your Power (send unconditional love) to each of the 50 trillion cells that make up your body – following the instructions in the chapter "You have a Superpower"

* Once you feel you've created the right feeling and you've aimed it at each of those amazing individual cells all doing their utmost to benefit the whole (you), then imagine that energy - the unconditional love - as a gold light, which has now completely saturated every part of you, every single cell. Next, imagine that Gold Light starting to expand out, filling the room, then the building, then the world, and finally the day ahead. LOVE that Thursday or Friday, or whatever day it is. Love it unconditionally. Love that day ahead, regardless of what it holds for you.

* If the module is still running after you've done this, take that Power - that unconditional love - and aim it at one situation/ issue/ person you've been concerned about. Remember, as mentioned in the original post, keep the love unconditional.

So, for example, I was worried about phoning someone. I was worried about a particular outcome from that phone call. When I sent this Power, this unconditional love, I tuned into the feeeeeling that I loved that phone call and the person on the other end - regardless of the result. Even if the result I was worried about occurred, I loved it and I loved that person - just for existing. (and it will ALWAYS - as long as you keep that love unconditional no matter what happens - it will ALWAYS turn out good, even if it's not the "good" you imagined. It may be something you'd never have thought of.)

Now, if you haven't done this before, it might sound impossible or far-fetched, but I assure you it is ABSOLUTELY possible. It only takes practice. It's as impossible as learning to walk, or learning to ride a bicycle or to drive a car, or to swim - or anything else that at first seems too hard.... and just takes practice.

* Now, go back to: http://www.paths-lifeboost.com scroll down and click on "Click here and try it FREE!" - "Increased Synchronicity - Amplified Awareness"

* Do the same as you did for the first one, and this time, once you've sent the unconditional love to your cells, try aiming it at something else - a loved one, or another issue that's concerning you. Remember UNCONDITIONAL - the Power is in the Unconditional bit. When you slip off the bicycle seat of unconditional love and feel an attachment to a particular outcome, your bike has fallen over - you need to straighten it up again (focus on unconditional - Love whatever or whoever it is just for existing - Regardless of any outcomes - you'll feel the difference)

This is your Daily Exercise. It will only take about 7 minutes - each module is only about 3 minutes. The modules will help with focus, as well as the other benefits you get from them - and they will also amplify your unconditional love.

Then.....

For these 7 days, make the commitment to change the way you react to things - Just for these 7 days. So, when it feels difficult, remind yourself "Okay, it's only for 7 days. Then I'll go back to reacting the old way." And know that at the end of 7 days, if you want to, you can just go back to your old ways. But of course, if you've seen results and you want to continue, then you can choose to do that too. ;)

So, here's how you're going to react differently for these 7 days: When something happens that upsets you, frustrates you, worries you, or even just mildly irritates you.... even something as minor as - it's pouring with rain (my own experience from yesterday here lol), and it's supposed to be summer, and it's miserable weather... your initial and instinctual reaction might be (as mine was) oh for goodness sake! I'm so sick of this rain! What ridiculous weather..... At this point you're going to catch yourself, conjure up that unconditional love you practiced this morning - conjure it up for your cells first, I find that's the easiest way ... or if something else works for you, for example you could conjure it up first for a loved one, pet, activity you love - whatever tunes you in.... and then AIM it at the weather. It only takes a moment. Change your language from "I'm so sick of this weather" to "I Love you" - with a cheeky smile on your face. A sense of humor helps. ;)

Do this with everything that comes up in your day. And whenever you think of it (you could put a sticky note reminder for yourself on the back of the bathroom door, your computer monitor or the fridge), focus unconditional love on all your cells. Practice it, and become familiar with the feeling - you'll feel it physically when it's spot on.

Finally....

Think of something that would make you beside yourself with excitement. For example, winning the lottery, a date with a certain person, a specific opportunity - the type of thing that, if it happened today, not only would you be ecstatic, but that when you woke up tomorrow morning, and remembered it, you'd have that experience all over again. The sort of thing that you would remind yourself of during the day because it would be just so incredible you'd have to remind yourself that it's real.

Pick a phrase that you would use in that case - like "I've won the lottery" or "Peter's asked me out" or "I got that contract" - and whatever it is, practice saying it, and conjuring up the feeling of excitement you would genuinely get in that situation.

Again, this takes practice, and sometimes the feeling will be spot on and sometimes you won't be able to conjure it up. Just keep practicing it. When you get it, you'll feel it physically - and it will be too much to keep up for very long at first. But with practice, you'll be able to extend the time. Do this whenever you think of it, and it will eventually become a habit .... and do you see then what the result is..... it is becoming a HABIT to vibrate in the same frequency with what you want - it is becoming a habit to vibrate in sync with exactly the feeeeling you're wanting to achieve... and then... (and this is from my own VERY Powerful experience) .. even while you're waiting for that specific desire to manifest, things you'd never have imagined will appear - which ALSO cause you to have that same reaction. It really is magic.

Here are some tips:

* Practice, practice, practice - this really does take practice. It helps to remember learning something else that took practice, like riding a bicycle or driving a car, or playing an instrument... and sometimes you'll get it and sometimes you won't. But the key is: the times you don't get it - recognize that it's exactly like learning to ride a bicycle. When you go a few yards, and then you fall off.... do you give up and decide you can't ride a bike or that it's impossible to stay upright on two wheels anyway... or do you pick up the bike and just keep practicing until it becomes muscle memory - and I promise you that is exactly what will happen with this - it will become muscle memory, and you will eventually find yourself doing it Automatically! ☺

* When "bad" things happen during your day - aim that Power at them. But remember, it's Unconditional... so don't expect the "bad" things to turn out right - just love them regardless (and as mentioned before, tune into that Power by using your cells or a loved one or a pet, then, once you've got the feeling and you're tuned into it, THEN aim it at whatever the issue is).

* REMEMBER... things are often not what they appear - During this experiment, just because something appears to be "bad" doesn't mean it is - I've found that EVERYTHING, even the "bad" stuff, has turned out to be either good, or nothing to worry about.

Hey, it's only 7 days – it's worth a try, right? ;)

Non-Judgment Day – a Fun Challenge – Can You Do it?

Here's a challenge for those who would like to REALLY boost their power of creating good stuff in their lives. Are you able to go one full day without judging or criticizing anyone or anything? It's a Massive challenge for anyone human lol. I'm starting today - I've already caught myself on automatic judgment mode and it's only 7.25am lol.

The Goal: To go through one full day without judging or criticising anyone or anything (*starting with my spelling of criticizing ;)*)

The Method: Most of us will be in the habit of automatically judging and criticizing (it's part of being human of course), so the idea is to catch yourself in the moment and transform that judgment and criticism into acceptance, allowance, love, even admiration or amusement - something positive that diffuses the feelings of judgment.

No matter how long we manage to last without judging or criticizing (even if it's only bits of a day) - **every second of it is an improvement** to our usual vibrational state and will therefore be **improving our lives on a core level** anyway - **resulting in more of what we want** ☺

 PS: Look out particularly for SELF judgment and criticism - that can be particularly sneaky ;)

Tips for this challenge:

- Keep a record of how long you can last at a time, without judging or criticizing.
- You could also challenge a friend to join you in the experiment – it's more fun when you're doing it with someone.☺

- When you catch yourself judging or criticizing there's no need to wait until the next day. Just start again in the moment! The more you practice, the sooner you'll manage a whole day. ☺ Just change the feeling in the moment, and continue. ☺

- Humor is a great tool in this challenge, it can help diffuse criticism and judgment. For example: When I first did this challenge, I started adding after certain thoughts or comments "... Not that I'm judging" ;) For example, I was on hold to an electricity supplier one afternoon for 45 minutes (and still never got through - eventually had to hang up), and caught myself um ... well, judging really ;) When their automated voice said "Ask our representative about our new energy-saving package" I caught myself saying "What representative?!"... and then added "Not that I'm judging..." ;)

The Happiness Game

How long can you remain in a state of happiness, regardless of what happens around you? Time yourself. Watch something that makes you laugh, or read something that makes you feel good, or speak to a friend who uplifts you, then write down the time, and see how long you can make that feeling last no matter what happens in your day from then on.

Do this for a few days in a row, and see if you can increase the amount of time you can hold it for. You can see it as a game, or you can see it as learning a new skill – it's kinda like learning to ride a unicycle or balance on a narrow wall. Each time you fall off, get back on and try again, and you'll get better and better at it.☺

The 5 Day Power of Laughter Experiment

Just for five days, start your day with something that makes you laugh out loud – whether it's a funny book, an episode of a TV sitcom, one of the many hilarious articles and blogs online, or a Youtube video of your favorite stand-up comedian. Start your day with something that makes you laugh out loud… and then remind yourself of it throughout your day. See if it makes a difference to your life.

Conclusion

I hope you've found something in this book that will empower you and enable you to not only triumph over challenges in your life, but achieve all the improvements you want to make.

As I said in the introduction, not all of the information will make sense to, or resonate with, everyone, but hopefully there's enough variety here to make sure that everyone gets at least something that can help them change their life.

If you have any questions or need clarification on anything in this book, please feel free to pop in to my blog (you'll find the address at the end of the book, under Resources) – and I will answer any queries there.

In the meantime, look after yourself. Do read through this book again – or at least through the chapters that made sense to you – because you'll find that each time you read it, you'll discover something more and learn something extra. Things will become clearer the more you read and refer to what is written here. And certainly, when you're feeling down or going through a challenging time, please pick up this book and re-read a couple of the chapters – it WILL help.☺

Love and Light and Magic

Illusions xxx

References and Resources:

In this list you'll find references and resources – some of which I've referred to in this book, and a couple extra that I've included here for those who wish to explore the different topics further.

To read more from Klaas Joehle you can visit his website at:

http://livingonlove.com/

The Secret

http://thesecret.tv/

Abraham-Hicks

http://www.abraham-hicks.com/lawofattractionsource

Powerful Intentions Forums

http://www.powerfulintentions.org/

Masaru Emoto's Experiments with Water Crystals

http://www.masaru-emoto.net/english/ephoto.html

Bruce Lipton (Biology of Belief)

http://www.brucelipton.com

Reprogramming the subconscious mind

http://pathsmindenergetics.blogspot.co.uk

The Power of the Subconscious Mind

http://www.squidoo.com/powerofthesubconsciousmind

My Law of Attraction Blog

http://law-of-attraction-tools.blogspot.co.uk

Printed in Great Britain
by Amazon.co.uk, Ltd.,
Marston Gate.